PLANTS
for your home

by Peter Seabrook　　　*Cacti by T.C. Rochford*

Nº ISBN 0 903001 06-3

A keen gardener from boyhood, Peter Seabrook gained two years' practical experience before going to the Writtle Agricultural College where he obtained the College Diploma in Horticulture.

After National Service, which included a course in floristry, ten years were spent with Cramphorn Limited, the well known Chelmsford based company with nurseries, garden centres and shops throughout the South East of England. During this period he obtained the Royal Horticultural Society's National Diploma in Horticulture. An ardent supporter of the British Group of the International Garden Centre Association, he gained first hand knowledge of the gardening public's likes and dislikes through his experience as the Group's first field officer. His knowledge and experience in the relatively modern field of garden centres is second to none.

More than four years were spent with the Irish Peat Development Authority, working with the major glasshouse nursery companies in Guernsey, the South Coast of England and the Lea Valley. This glasshouse experience was further extended by his appointment as director of William Strike Limited, the Yorkshire and County Durham based company where he had the responsibility for cropping two commercial glasshouse nurseries with pot plants.

Although only his second complete book, Peter Seabrook writes regularly for the horticultural magazines, both amateur and professional, as well as taking part in radio and television broadcasts. His knowledge of the modern gardening scene and his commercial experience of indoor plant cultivation provided a fruitful source of information for this book.

It is this knowledge of indoor plants coupled with his awareness of the ordinary person's plant growing needs that makes 'Plants for your Home' a valuable addition to every bookshelf.

Thomas Christopher Rochford was born in 1947 and is the fourth Thomas Rochford to be associated with the family pot plant business. He studied classics at Ampleforth College in Yorkshire and took a degree in law at Cambridge in 1968. Subsequently he has worked in Germany and with the family business where he was responsible for setting up the highly successful range of Flowers from the Desert. After reading for a Diploma in Management Studies, he joined the Board of Thomas Rochford and Sons Limited in 1972 as Business Director on his Father's retirement.

Mr. Rochford is a director of Horticultural Exports (Great Britain) Ltd., a director of Elms Gardens Sales and a member of the Ornamentals Panel of A.C.M.S. Ltd.

The cover illustration shows a mixed bowl arrangement of Rhoicissus rhomboidea, Euphorbia pulcherrima ("Poinsettia"), Hypocyrta glabra, Hedera helix 'Glacier' and Peperomia magnoliaefolia 'Variegata'.

This bowl of plants contains Hedera canariensis 'Variegata', Codiaeum variegatum, Asplenium nidus, Peperomia caperata, Hedera helix 'Chicago', Saintpaulia
ionantha.

Abutilon

These shrubby plants will eventually grow several metres high but are not hardy and will be killed by frost. They are grown in pots for indoor decoration and may be planted in the garden during the summer months to give height to summer flowering bedding plant schemes. The large, palm-shaped leaves of *Abutilon x hybridum* are mid green and there are cultivars with white, cream and yellow variegated leaves and flowers in shades of red, yellow and orange.

Another popular species is *Abutilon megapotamicum*, with thinner, more arching and pendulant growth and slender sword-shaped leaves, *A.m.* 'Variegatum' has leaves mottled yellow. Both plants carry red and yellow flowers from May to September.

Very easy to grow, they thrive in John Innes Potting Compost No. 2 and other composts of similar fertiliser strength. A minimum temperature of 10°C (50°F) is required, as is some shade from very strong sun in high summer and a light window or glasshouse site through the winter.

Cuttings may be taken from early spring onwards but root more easily in summer and if the plants get to big for their position the main branches can be cut back by half in March and the side shoots cut back to 7½-10 cm.

ABUTILON x hybridum

ACALYPHA hispida

Acalypha hispida

The attractive common name "Red-hot Cat-tail" aptly describes the long tassel-shaped crimson flowers of *Acalypha hispida* although "Chenille Plant" is said to be the correct common name. Another tender shrubby plant which eventually reaches 3-5 m high, and while it can be used for 'sub-tropical' bedding like the *Abutilon* it is best grown indoors in pots with a minimum winter temperature of 15°C (60°F), minimum summer temperature of 20°C (70°F), ideally a moist atmosphere and a light position. There are other species with colourful nettle-like leaves and insignificant flowers but they are not freely available.

These plants grow well in John Innes and the soilless composts. If they outgrow the space available for them, cut back in February and March, which is also the best time for repotting and rooting cuttings. Propagation is by cuttings but a very warm temperature (80°F) is needed. This is the plant to grow in the heated sun lounge and greenhouse if you are looking for something a little different.

Achimenes

ACHIMENES

An old fashioned plant which is regaining its popularity because of the very free flowering new cultivars now available is the *Achimenes*.

They can be grown from the dry tuberous roots, which look rather like "Silver Birch" cones, and from cuttings taken in early spring. All *Achimenes* grow well in the proprietary peat composts, planting 4 to 6 tubers 2 cm deep or five cuttings to a 13 cm (5 in) pot. They need warmth and humidity until well budded. The older taller growing varieties are very attractive in hanging baskets, where the branches trail over the sides absolutely festooned with flower. Plant the corms and rooted cuttings 3-5 cm apart around the edge of the basket.

A temperature of 15°C (65°F) is required to start the tubers into growth and while a light position is needed to avoid tall, weak stems developing, the *Achimenes* should be shaded from direct hot sun in high summer. When the plants die down in the autumn dry the compost out and store in a frost free place until repotting and starting into growth the following March/April.

When the plants get too tall and the branches rather weak, pinch out the tip to encourage more bushy basal branching. A few twiggy sticks are also useful to support taller growing cultivars.

ACORUS gramineus variegatus

Acorus

The fleshy root and flat striped leaves of *Acorus gramineus variegatus* and are rather grass like in appearance. It grows 25 cm high and requires cool, moist conditions. Propagate this plant by division in spring and put into John Innes Potting Compost No. 1.

The *Acorus* species are hardy plants and low room temperatures are acceptable. If you are looking for something to stand shade, cold and some over watering this could well be your plant. It grows well in bottle gardens and terrariums but may eventually get a little large and need dividing because the tips of the leaves may turn brown when they touch the glass.

ADIANTUM raddianum

Adiantum

One of the most popular of all ferns is the "Maidenhair", with delicate soft green fronds carried on wiry black stems. Whilst there are several hardy forms grown in gardens it is the *Adiantum raddianum*, syn. *A. cuneatum*, which is the popular house plant and its cultivars, like the scented-leaved *A.r.* 'Fragrantissimum' the longer fronded *A.r.* 'Fritz Luthii' and pinkish young leaves of *A.r.* 'Scutum Roseum'.

All the indoor "Maidenhair Ferns" grow well in all peat potting composts and are best transplanted and repotted in March/April. They require a light position but away from strong direct sunlight in high summer, so a north window is ideal. A cool damp atmosphere is the best and a temperature not below 10°C (50°F) throughout the year. If low temperatures do occur the plants lose their leaves but produce new growth in the spring.

The secret with these plants is to find a situation and treatment that suits them and then leave undisturbed. Given this, they will flourish for years. A dry atmosphere, fluctuating temperature and over watering, especially in the winter, are death to these plants.

While large plants can be divided, it is wiser to start again with young spore-raised plants if your specimen has become too large for its situation. If you have a frost free greenhouse, try a few plants under staging, they will thrive there.

ADIANTUM raddianum 'Fragrantissimum'

Aechmea

AECHMEA fasciata

The 'Bromeliads', members of the "Pineapple" family, include a number of attractive and popular house plants. One of the longest lasting flowers of all flowering house plants is *Aechmea fasciata,* also known as *A. rhodocyanea* and *Billbergia rhodocyanea.* The large plump flower head emerges from a circle of leaves with typical sawtooth edges. These grey-green leaves form an open vase shape and account for the common name "Greeek Vase Plant".

These plants grow to 60 cm (24 in) and ideally require a temperature of 16°C (60°F). If care is taken not to over water, especially in the winter, lower temperatures will be survived. During the summer and in dry atmospheres the plant welcomes the occasional leaf spray with water and the centre of the 'vase' should be kept topped up with water throughout the year. Lime-free composts are required and the use of rainwater and soft water is preferable. While the plants are best in a light sunny position, they will survive shade. In fact they really are tough house plants.

In modern office surroundings and in collections of plants in modern containers the Aechmea is most attractive. While the size of pot is modest in comparison with the top growth, the plants look best in a bold modern pot plant cover and even better in a cork bark surround.

An interesting and colourful collection of house plants.

AGLAONEMA treubii

AGLAONEMA picta

Aglaonema

Commonly called "Silver Spear", the *Aglaonema treubii* and one of the newer hybrids *A.* 'Silver Queen' are grown for their attractive leaves, although the yellow green flower spathes of *A. pictum* and white spathes followed by dark red berries of *A. treubii* are an added attraction. The "Chinese Evergreen", *A. commutatum*, is very popular in the States but for some extraordinary reason it has not caught on in Britain.

All the *Aglaonema* thrive in warm, moist and shaded conditons and where some extra moisture can be introduced to the atmosphere, by standing the pots in a bowl of damp peat for example, they are good house plants. A minimum winter temperature of 10°C (50°F) is required and care should be taken not to overwater in the winter. Growth will be better with 16°C (60°F) temperatures. These plants grow

some 16 cm (6 in) high and spread to 30 cm (12 in) or more. A monthly dilute liquid feed through the summer will keep new foliage coming and strengthen the leaf colour.

Plants are propagated by taking basal shoots with several leaves and roots in April/May. These are potted up into all peat potting composts and 13 cm (5 in) pots. Keep the newly potted offsets warm, 18-20°C (65-70°F) until well established.

Established plants can be moved on into larger pots in April, repotting every second year. Once plants fill a 16 cm (6 in) pot it is probably best to start again with young, more vigorous growing plants.

Try these plants in mixed groups where a good canopy of leaf colour is required in a position with some light but away from direct sunshine.

8

Allamanda

Whilst in natural surroundings the *Allamanda* is an evergreen climber, by the occasional pinching out of leading shoots they make attractive bushy pot plants. The best form is *Allamanda cathartica* 'Grandiflora', which has pale yellow trumpet flowers from July to September and if the shoots are stopped when 24-32 cm (9-12 in) long, plants some 60 cm (24 in) in height and width are produced.

They require a minimum temperature of 13°C (55°F) and need to be kept on the dry side through the winter. In spring and summer when growing strongly give them plenty of water and a liquid feed every 10 to 14 days. Because of their vigorous growth repotting is necessary every April, using John Innes Potting Compost No. 3. If you have the space, in, say a sun lounge or lean-to greenhouse, then pot on eventually into 48 cm (18 in) tubs. An alternative suggestion is to either plant in border soil under glass or grow in tubs and let them climb but allow some 3 m. (9 ft) or more head room.

New plants are propagated by taking cuttings 8 cm (3 in) long of the previous year's growth in April. A temperature of 24°C (75°F) is needed for rapid rooting.

This is just the plant to bring a touch of tropical vegetation to the conservatory and glass-sided home extension. If the plant gets out of hand, then prune the previous year's growth back to within one or two leaves of the old wood in February.

ALLAMANDA cathartica

AMPELOPSIS brevipedunculata elegans

Ampelopsis

One of the few plants described in this book which is deciduous and loses its leaves in winter, the *Ampelopsis brevipedunculata*, also known as *A. heterophylla elegans*, comes from the group of plants commonly referred to as "Virginia Creeper". This plant is best suited to the temperate greenhouse and when in full growth can be brought indoors where it will stand quite cool conditions throughout the summer before loosing its leaves.

All composts are suitable and John Innes No. 1 Potting Compost is recommended. Plants can be repotted in spring and growth is better where the atmosphere is not too dry. New plants are propagated from cuttings in summer. A good plant for the glass sided porch and sun lounge where loss of leaf in winter is acceptable.

Ananas

The "Pineapple", both the ordinary green leaved *Ananas sativus* and the brightly variegated *Ananas sativus* 'Variegatus', sometimes called *A. comosus* and *A. comosus* 'Variegatus' respectively and *A. bracteatus striatus*', make very interesting and attractive house plants. The variegated forms are especially pretty with the broad cream to white bands of variegation and the more spectacular red spines and edible fruit of *A.b. striatus.*

Given ample space and sufficient root run these plants will reach from 1-1.5 m (3-5 ft) in the ideal winter growing temperature of 18-20°C (65-70°F). Restricting the roots in 13-15 cm (5-6 in) pots and growing at cooler temperature restricts the size. A light position is needed, full sunlight if the richest colour is to be obtained from the variegated form.

Occasionally spraying the leaves with water, especially in summer, is an advantage and the plants need much more water in summer. It is wise to let the plants dry out between watering rather than keep the compost permanently wet.

ANANAS sativus 'Variegatus'

ANANAS bracteatus striatus

ANANAS sativus fruiting

ANTHURIUM scherzerianum

Anthurium

The quite remarkable flowers of *Anthurium*, looking like an opened up arum lily, are very long lasting, both on the plant and when cut and placed in water. Grown as pot plants they are seldom out of flower. There is only one species which will stand the dry atmosphere in homes, namely *A. scherzerianum* and commonly called "Flamingo Flower". Pots of this plant are better placed in a bowl filled with damp peat to provide humidity. It will survive temperatures as low as 10°C (50°F) but 16°C (61°F) is a more acceptable minimum. Other species with larger and more spectacular flowers will certainly require the higher temperature. If the temperature is too low the leaf edges turn yellow. Under normal house conditions *A. scherzerianum* will reach 22 cm (9 in) high and 36 cm (in) spread.

It's main flowering period is from January onwards and they grow best in the all-peat potting composts, ideally improved for *Anthurium* by the addition of one part chopped sphagnum moss to three parts of compost. House plants are best kept in the 13 cm (5 in) size of pot and when potting see the crown of the plant stands above the surface. When new roots appear at the crown cover with a top dressing of moss and/or peat.

Plants are increased by division in April, the best time to repot and provide some fresh compost for established plants. Rain water or soft tap water is adviseable and dilute liquid feeding once a fortnight through the summer is required by established plants. This is a plant to grow more for its unusual appearance than its overall attractive form.

Aphelandra

Few plants are more striking than the rich dark green leaves striped white and bold yellow bracts and flowers of *Aphelandra squarrosa* 'Louisae' and the improved cultivar *A.s.* 'Dania', with more compact growth and shorter leaves. The ivory marking along the mid-rib and side veins, in marked contrast to the dark green, has given rise to the common name "Zebra Plant". The yellow bracts remain as a bright spike while the yellow flowers develop and die, providing a very long supply of colour.

Two requirements are necessary for healthy plants, steady moisture levels, not too wet and not too dry, and warmth, a minimum winter temperature of 10°C (55°F). If you let the plant dry the leaves drop from the horizontal position and stay hanging down. One way of maintaining the compost nicely damp but not too wet is to stand the pot on a saucer filled with fine sand. Water the plant once from the top and then keep the sand damp, leaving the plant to draw the moisture it needs by capillarity. Higher temperatures than the minimum, say 16°C (61°F) also make plant care easier.

This plant is very worthwhile and once established in a light position away from direct sunshine in the summer, will give great pleasure. After flowering the shoot should be cut back to just above the first good pair of leaves below the dying bract and new shoots will grow from the stem.

Repotting is best done in March using John Innes Potting Compost No. 2 and the 13 cm (5 in) pot is adequate for indoor plants.

APHELANDRA squarrosa 'Dania'

ARAUCARIA excelsa compacta

Araucaria

Choose the "Norfolk Island Pine", *Araucaria excelsa compacta*, if you want a really easy house plant with attractive whorls of typically flat pine tree branches. This plant is almost hardy and will grow outside in warm maritime areas. It grows eventually 1-2 m (3-6 ft) high and spreads to 1 m (3 ft). A minimum winter temperature of 5°C (41°F) will be survived.

Either John Innes Potting Compost No. 2 or a peat compost of similar richness should be used when potting into larger pots in March, fully mature specimens being grown in 20-25 cm (8-10 in) pots. *Araucaria* will withstand shade — not too dark though — and most room conditions, although if very dry the occasional water spray over the leaves is helpful. Keep just damp through the winter and water freely in summer, giving a dilute liquid feed once a month.

If you wish, this plant can be stood outside through the summer and indoors it makes a fine specimen.

Aspidistra

Perhaps the toughest of all indooor plants is the *Aspidistra* and certainly the plant with the reputation for being tough, to the point of a common name "Cast Iron Plant". Best known is the green leaved *A. elatior* and brighter in appearance is the variegated cream and green leaved *A.e.* 'Variegata'.

While they tolerate intense shade, fluctuating temperatures and dry atmospheres, really rich foliage comes from better cultural conditions. An ideal temperature is 10-15°C (50°-60°F), although they survive much lower temperatures, and plants should be repotted every second or third year in March, using a compost to the strength of John Innes No. 2. They grow best in light shade and require regular watering through the summer with a monthly dilute liquid feed. Keep the compost just damp through the winter and wash the leaves occasionally to remove dust and freshen the plants up.

Plants are propagated by division in March and April. If you are known to forget your plants the *Aspidistra* should be in your collection, happily surviving the occasional severe drought.

ASPIDISTRA elatior

ASPIDISTRA elatior 'Variegata'

Asparagus

Feathery and attractive rich green foliage are the qualities which make the *Asparagus* species suited to indoor culture so popular. The fact that branches can be cut and arranged in water with flowers increases their usefulness. While the two main forms *Asparagus plumosus* and *Asparagus sprengeri*, given a free root run, produce trailing twining stems of 1 m and more long, in pots they form attractive well balanced plants.

They are easy plants to grow even in quite shaded positions indoors. Once established they take quite a lot of water through the summer and a dilute liquid feed every ten days improves the growth and appearance. The compost should be kept just moist through the winter, especially if the minimum winter temperatures of 7°C (45°F) are experienced.

Once the plants outgrow the 13 cm (5 in) pots they are better either replaced by new seedlings raised from April sown seed or planted in hanging baskets to decorate the sun lounge and greenhouse. Large plants can be divided but better growth and shape is more easily achieved by starting with young seed raised stock. Both the soil based and proprietary peat composts to John Innes No. 1 strength are recommended for *Asparagus*. Do not be afraid to try the hanging basket idea, even mixing with flowering annuals and geraniums in the summer.

ASPARAGUS *sprengeri*

ASPARAGUS *plumosus*

Asplenium

The rich green leaves, from 15 cm (6 in) to 60 cm (24 in) long, of *Asplenium nidus*, the "Bird's-nest Fern", make a most attractive house plant. It can be used as a specimen and in association with other plants. This plant is excellent for bottle gardens and terrariums if the container is large enough and, alternatively, if you are prepared to replace when the leaves get too large.

They grow well in the all-peat composts and require a light position, out of strong direct sunlight, and a minimum winter temperature of 10°C (50°F). Repot in April using up to the 13 cm (5 in) pot for most indoor purposes. Larger pots will produce the maximum leaf size which can be excessive for some houses.

Easier to grow, almost hardy and more interesting than attractive is *Asplenium bulbiferum*, so named because of the small plantlets which form on the mature leaves. While the "Bird's-nest Fern" is more difficult to propagate, being raised from spores, *A. bulbiferum* is easily increased by pulling off young plantlets from the mature fronds and potting them up anytime of the year and preferably in late spring and early summer.

Water freely during the rapid growing period of late spring and summer and keep the compost just nicely damp for the rest of the year.

ASPLENIUM nidus

AUCUBA japonica 'Crotonifolia'

Aucuba

The *Aucuba japonica* is a very popular, hardy evergreen shrub widely grown in gardens. Several variegated leaf forms, of which *Aucuba japonica* 'Crotonifolia' is a good example, can be grown indoors as house plants. We have the added advantage that if these plants outgrow the space available for them indoors they can be moved to the garden.

Plants are produced from rooted cuttings and grown in all composts of John Innes Potting Compost No. 2 strength, doing any annual repotting in March/April. They thrive in partial shade indoors but the compost needs to be kept moist at all times and the leaves occasionally washed to remove dust. A dilute liquid feed every three weeks from May to September speeds the growth. Don't forget, these plants are hardy and are best in cool room conditions, they are excellent subjects to decorate window boxes outside, especially in the winter when colourful evergreen subjects are so valuable.

AZALEA 'Blushing Bride', ''Indian Azalea''

AZALEA 'Perfect', ''Japanese Azalea''

Azalea

The correct botanical name is *Rhododendron simsii* and *Rhododendron* cultivars but most of us prefer the names *Azalea indicum* and more commonly ''Indian Azaleas''. They are among the most attractive and floriferous indoor plants but will not stand frost. These plants are produced commercially as attractive bushy specimens to be forced into early flower by providing a temperature of 13-15°C (55-60°F) from November onwards. The majority of these forced plants are offered in flower from Christmas to Easter but recent cultural techniques are providing almost year round flowering.

Three things are needed to get the maximum decorative life from the Azalea once in flower; a cool temperature, 13°C (55°F), light position and sufficient moisture. Watering should be with lime-free water, either rain water or the condensate from the 'fridge. A very good guide to the water needs of a single stemmed pot grown *Azalea* can be seen on the stem at compost level. If the compost is sufficiently damp there will be a dark mark (caused by moisture) on the bottom 2 cm (0.8 in) of stem. If this wet mark is less than 1 cm (0.4 in) the plant will need watering and if over 2 cm (0.8 in) it has been overwatered and must be left to dry. If plants have been allowed to get very dry, plants in this state are very light weight when lifted up, it is best to plunge the pot in water until no air bubbles appear and then the plant should be stood to drain before returning to the window sill.

It is not too easy to get the ''Indian Azaleas'' into flower for a second year but the method to achieve this is to continue watering and giving the occasional liquid feed until April/May. When outside conditions are mild, that is, no sign of frost, harden the plants to outside conditions and plunge the pots in soil. A shady position in early summer helps the plants to recover from forced flowering and a spell in late summer in full sunshine helps ripen the wood and set flower bud in the tips of the shoots. Syringe the plants regularly with water and see that the compost never gets dry. Bring indoors before the frost in September.

The ''Japanese Azalea'', whilst not quite so attractive in flower form as the best *A. indicum*, has the advantage that it is hardy and can be planted in the garden after flowering indoors. These *Azalea* species will not stand the higher temperatures and they flower in March/April if brought indoors early February and kept at 13°C (55°F). Good cultivars for indoors and the garden are 'Hino-Crimson', 'Mothers Day' and 'Rosebud'.

AZALEA 'Schnee'

AZALEA 'Perle de Noisy'

AZALEA 'Ambrosius'

AZALEA 'Findeisen'

AZALEA 'Else Kärger'

AZALEA 'Ambrosiana'

17

Begonia

BEGONIA 'Marina' a "Lorraine Begonia"

There are some 900 different species of *Begonia* and an ever increasing number of hybrids to confuse the indoor gardener. All require warm temperatures, a light situation — invariably better out of strong direct sunlight — and, ideally, a humid atmosphere. Some of the more recent hybrids withstand quite harsh indoor conditions, however, and are excellent house plants. While the species are unisexual, carrying male and female flowers, some of the hybrids are sterile and flower for ever in the vain attempt at reproduction.

Three groups according to root formation allow some classification of this large collection; the fleshy creeping roots of the rhizomatous types, the bulb forming tuberous types and the fibrous rooted types. Hybrids blur the lines of distinction between these three.

BEGONIA masoniana

Rhizomatous Begonias

The most popular examples in this group are *Begonia rex* and *Begonia masoniana*, the latter commonly called "Begonia Iron Cross". Both are grown for their attractively coloured foliage with the "Iron Cross" having a puckered, bristly surface to the leaves and definite deep bronze iron cross mark. If grown in too shaded a position the leaf colourings fade.

They require a minimum winter temperature of 13°C (55°F), 16°C (61°F) through the summer and a light position out of direct sunlight. A moist atmosphere keeps these plants happy and to achieve this in the home either group the *Begonia* species with other plants or plant in glass containers of the bottle garden, terrarium type. Keep the soil just moist through the winter and occasionally syringe the leaves in summer.

Repotting is best done in April and strong growth is made in the peat composts, although all proprietary composts give acceptable results. Large plants can be divided at the time of repotting and new plants are obtained from small sections of mature leaves cut out to the size of a postage stamp and rooted in warm moist conditions.

Hybrids

Increasing in importance are the hybrids from tuberous rooted species which flower in mid winter. Among these the "Lorraine Begonias", for example *Begonia* x 'Gloire de Lorraine' and *Begonia* x 'Marina' are well known. 'Gloire de Lorraine' has a fibrous root system and some similar hybrids have a more tuberous root.

These winter flowering hybrids are not easy to keep the year round, they require a light position, especially in winter, out of direct sunlight, a damp atmosphere and a minimum winter temperature of 15°C (61°F), avoiding fiercely fluctuating temperatures. Propagation is by rooted cuttings in the spring.

Further breeding work on one winter flowering hybrid, *Begonia* 'Elatior' has resulted in a range of very free flowering cultivars referred to as "Elatior",

BEGONIA rex, four plants illustrating range of leaf colour

"Europa" and "Rieger" Begonias. They flower all the year round, make excellent house plants and look especially attractive under artificial light. The large single flowers have a bright yellow contrasting centre and popular varieties include *B.* x 'Schwabenland' and *B.* x 'Fireglow', both brilliant scarlet and virtually indistinguishable, and *B.* x 'Appleblossom', soft pink.

Where the day length is 14 hours and over these new hybrids make vegetative growth and with less than 14 hours of light in 24 they produce flower buds. The ideal temperature is a steady 18°C (64°F) and they grow well in all peat and peat enriched composts. Very occasional liquid feeding during the summer is all they require and if plants get too tall and straggly just cut them back and new growth comes from the base.

Mildew, the soft white growth on leaves and Botrytis, a wet brown rot, occur under conditions of cool, too dark and too damp conditions. Where the room is shut up and has no air movement, for example when the family is on holiday, the speed of mildew spread increases. A spray with Benlate (a benomyl based material) quickly clears up these two diseases.

Fibrous Begonias

Easiest of all indoor flowering plants and perhaps too widely known because of their excellent summer flowering qualities grown for bedding, are *Begonia semperflorens* hybrids. There are both green and rich chocolate coloured leaved cultivars. The dark leaved white flowering types are especially attractive and the full flower colour range is white, pink and red.

Following extensive breeding work we have many F_1 hybrids which are raised from seed in spring. The seed is very small and requires warm conditions, 20°C (70°F), for good germination. Once established they grow strongly in all composts and will stand a fair degree of shade. You can even lift and pot up plants from the garden in the autumn before frost and they make excellent flowering subjects right through the winter. The red flowering cultivars look good at Christmas. These F_1 hybrids, although raised from seed are themselves sterile and flower for ever with no chance of setting seed. While plants can be propagated from cuttings new stock from seed is the recommended way to grow them. If you have a loved specimen in a pot and it has become over sized, just cut it back and new growth quickly comes from the base.

BEGONIA x 'Schwabenland'

Tuberous Begonias

Best known of all Begonias is *Begonia x tuberhybrida,* the kind grown easily from fleshy tubers, 1-5 cm (½-2 in) across, sold in the shops each spring. Great big saucer sized double flowers are the envy of every casual passer-by at summer flower shows the world over. For all practical purposes there are but two kinds, both with typical begonia leaves and succulent, fleshy stems, one upright with very large flowers and the second with smaller flowers and very many more of them of upright and pendulus habit.

Whilst these plants can be overwatered, the big danger occurs when they get dry because this causes the flowers to drop.

They can be grown outside in beds, borders and window boxes as well as indoors in pots and all sites can be damp, partially shaded situations. They must be kept free from frost at all times and the secret of success is very warm temperatures 21°C (70°F) to start the tubers into growth. I like to put the tubers in a polythene bag with damp peat and place in the airing cupboard or similar warm spots in spring. Once roots and shoots appear they can be potted up in rich compost to John Innes No. 2 strength, the all peat composts are very good, using a 9 cm (3½ in) pot initially and then into 13 cm (5 in) pots for flowering. A summer temperature of 15°C (61°F) is required.

Six weeks from final potting liquid feed once every two weeks. The removal of single female flowers increases flower size and extends the period of flowering. Once flowering has finished in the autumn lie the pots on their sides to dry out and then store the tubers in frost free conditions until the following spring. Plants are propagated from seed and by taking cuttings, even by cutting very large tubers in half once they have started into growth and at least two separate shoots are clearly visible.

The Pendula types are excellent subjects for window boxes and hanging baskets as well as for indoor decoration in pots.

BEGONIA x tuberhybrida — Pendula type — note double (male) and single (female) flowers

BEGONIA x tuberhybrida

BELOPERONE guttata

Beloperone

The common name "Shrimp Plant", for *Beloperone guttata*, refers to the dull shrimp pink bracts of the arching flower sprays. There is a less commonly offered variety with green and yellow bracts and flower. Because colour comes from the bracts, as well as the protruding white flowers, the plants are interesting and colourful for a very long period. They are very easy to grow, standing cool conditions with a minimum temperature requirement of 7°C (45°F).

All pot plant growing mediums are suitable and plants of various sizes can be produced indoors, the size of plant depending on pot size, with 9 cm (3½ in) pots for the smallest plants and really attractive plants being grown in 14-20 cm (6-8 in) pots. When the plants get straggly and bare at the base prune back in spring by one half to encourage new basal growth.

New plants are produced by rooting cuttings of non flowering shoots in spring. Young plants are more attractive and easier to keep attractive than old woody stock. Keep the plant a bit on the dry side through the winter and the Beloperone thrives on sunny window sills. If flowering plants are moved to the more shaded centre of rooms, give them a holiday every now and then on the sunny window sill to allow recuperation.

Excellent plants for use in troughs of assorted indoor plants and as specimens. The smaller plants look best in association with other indoor plants and the flower colour blends naturally without exception. Grown outside in containers as summer patio plants, they take on a very intense colour and are very attractive when used in this way.

Blechnum

Generally speaking, the tougher shiny leaved ferns are the easiest for indoor cultivation and *Blechnum gibbum* is no exception. A short thick stump almost like a tree develops as this fern ages. While not freely available, this plant grows well out of direct sunlight and in partial shade. It requires a minimum temperature of 10°C (50°F) and grows well in the all peat potting composts. The occasional wiping of the leaves with a damp cloth and syringing with rain water helps provide the damp atmosphere preferred by ferns.

Propagation of plants is from spores, a demanding job best left to the specialist. Potting plants on into larger containers is best done in spring and water should be given freely through the spring, summer and autumn, the compost kept just damp in winter.

BLECHNUM gibbum

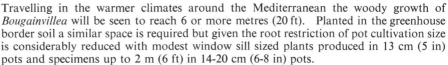
BOUGAINVILLEA glabra

Bougainvillea

Travelling in the warmer climates around the Mediterranean the woody growth of *Bougainvillea* will be seen to reach 6 or more metres (20 ft). Planted in the greenhouse border soil a similar space is required but given the root restriction of pot cultivation size is considerably reduced with modest window sill sized plants produced in 13 cm (5 in) pots and specimens up to 2 m (6 ft) in 14-20 cm (6-8 in) pots.

The flowers are small and insignificant, it is the tissue-paper thin bracts surrounding the flowers which provide the brilliant colour in spring and early summer. *Bougainvillea glabra* has purple bracts and although a vigorous growing climber, it flowers when quite young. The hybrid *B. x buttiana* 'Killie Campbell' has orange bracts.

A minimum frost free temperature of 7 °C (45 °F) is required and a compost of John Innes No. 3 richness the ideal. The plants are either pinched to retain size or trained up canes and wires. Established specimens require a dilute liquid feed once a fortnight in spring and summer and regular watering at this time. After flowering the watering is gradually reduced and the compost kept almost dry through the winter until growth is restarted in March. For the best results a warm, sunny position is needed, especially in spring and summer.

Pruning consists of shortening the lead growths by one third and cutting all side shoot growth back to within 2.5 cm (1 in) of the main stems in February. New plants are propagated from cuttings taken in summer but a high temperature, at least 21 °C (70 °F) is required.

A whole range of hybrids are available covering the colours from orange through yellow to white. Two recent introductions have double bracts, which remain on the plant without dropping for a longer period, and are known as *B.* 'Dania' one is red the other pink.

Caladium

The charming common name "Angel's Wings", adequately describes the beautiful paper thin leaves of *Caladium bicolor.* A native of tropical South America, this plant is a good one for those of us who tend to overwater as it requires ample moisture during the period of rapid growth in spring and early summer. It is grown from Tubers, pieces of fleshy root, started into growth in spring by placing in damp peat at a temperature of 21°C (70°F). Once growth starts put 2½ cm (1 in) deep in a free draining material like John Innes No. 2 potting compost. Small tubers are potted one to a 13 cm (5 in) pot, larger tubers one to a 17 cm (6 in) pot. Dull green typical arum flower spathes are produced in summer usually just before the period of dormancy but they are insignificant and the full beauty is in the leaves.

Once well established the temperature can be dropped, the leaves hardened and plants are then ready for indoor decoration. Place in a draught free situation away from strong direct sunlight, do not use too shady a position, however, as this reduces leaf colour. When the leaves die down in late summer reduce watering and keep the pots just damp and in a temperature of 13°C (55°F) until starting the tubers into growth the following spring. Plants are increased by dividing up the tubers in spring.

Beautiful plants to use as specimens, when stood at floor and lower levels to be looked down on they are most attractive. They are best set against a green background, and if this green background is foliage plants the humidity is increased and this suits the *Caladium.*

CALADIUM bicolor

CALADIUM bicolor 'Candidum'

CALADIUM bicolor 'Stoplight'

Calceolaria

There are several attractive common names for the *Calceolaria x herbeo-hybrida,* all of which refer to the soft velvety pouched flowers. Two good examples are "Slipper Flower" and "Pocket Book Flower". A cool 7-10°C (45-50°F) light window sill is all you require for this plant, in fact if the temperature goes over 15°C (60°F) the flower buds will not form. Strong, hot sunlight in late spring shortens the flower life of this plant.

Several strains exist, the taller ones growing to 45 cm (18 in) and the dwarf ones 24-30 cm (9-12 in), all having flowers in shades of yellow, orange and red, the majority spotted and blotched crimson. Plants are raised from seed sown from June to October to flower late in the following spring and early summer. Size of plant is to some extent controlled by pot size, with larger specimens grown in 13-15 cm (5-6 in) pots. Both John Innes Potting Compost No. 2 and the proprietary peat composts give good results.

Be very sparing with the water mid winter, increasing the amount as the day length and speed of growth increases. True biennials, sown one year to flower the next, they should be discarded once flowering has finished.

Thus *Calceolaria* is an excellent plant for sun lounges, glass porches and glass sided home extensions where the temperature is cool but frost free and light through the winter.

CALCEOLARIA x herbeo-hybrida

CALCEOLARIA x herbeo-hybrida

CALCEOLARIA x herbeo-hybrida

Callistemon

CALLISTEMON *citrinus*

Shrubby growth reaching in time more than 2 metres (6 ft) makes the "Bottle Brush Tree" from Australia a somewhat different kind of flowering house plant. The cylindrical whorls of flower in mid summer and evergreen leaves are attractive and of value where sufficient space is available.

The *Callistemon citrinus* will need a 25-30 cm (10-12 in) pot and compost of John Innes No. 2 Potting Compost strength. Repotting is best done in April. A light position, preferably full sun, is needed with a minimum winter temperature of 7°C (45°F). Plants can be stood outside on the patio and terrace in summer and all the year in very sheltered districts which are free of winter frost.

Propagation is by cuttings taken in summer but plenty of warmth and the facilities of a propagating frame are needed. An excellent plant for the sun lounge and glass sided porch which are just kept frost free through the winter. Dwarf flowering forms of *Callistemon* sold in florist shops have been treated with growth retardent. Normal growth will ensue the following year after repotting.

Camellia

Perfectly hardy and able to withstand quite severe frost, *Camellia japonica* is another plant which can be used indoors and in the garden. The only problem out of doors is that hard winter weather damages the exotic wax-like flowers carried in early spring, especially in east facing situations. There are many excellent forms with double, semi-double and single flowers in colours from white to pink and red.

The best way to cultivate these plants is to grow in pots, the pots plunged in soil in the garden to help keep them moist through the late spring, summer and early autumn, to bring indoors for winter and early spring. When brought indoors they need a cool, ideally 7-10°C (45-50°F) temperature and on no account should the compost be allowed to dry out. Too high a temperature and dryness causes the flower buds to drop.

They require lime-free soil and watering should be with rainwater, the presence of lime will cause yellowing of the leaves. Composts containing a high proportion of peat give good growth. They are excellent plants for tubs but because of their hardiness can stand outside the whole year.

CAMELLIA *japonica*

CAMELLIA *japonica* 'Mathotiana Rubra'

CAMELLIA x *williamsii* 'Donation'

Campanula

There are hundreds of different *Campanula* species, many of them good garden plants and one, *Campanula isophylla*, is a charming pot plant. Grown naturally it trails and is an excellent subject for pots in wall brackets and hanging containers. Given careful pinching out of the growing tips in the spring and the support of twiggy sticks or split cane, compact upright plants full of flower are produced similar to the specimen illustrated.

Masses of sky blue flowers cover the plant in summer and early autumn, there is an equally attractive and slightly larger white flowered form *C. i.* 'Alba'. Almost hardy these plants, commonly called "Star of Bethlehem", grow best in a cool 10°C (50°F) moist atmosphere. They need to be kept just frost free and on the dry side through the winter and are propagated from cuttings taken in spring. Where flowering plants in pots are placed on window sills in summer they should be kept out of direct hot sunlight. They grow well in the soil based John Innes Potting Compost No. 1.

Two cultivars of the completely hardy perennial *Campanula carpatica* are also good pot plants, *C. c.* 'Blue Chips', pure light blue and *C. c.* 'White Chips' will stand frost. They are raised from seed in May, grown without heat through the summer and given the protection of an unheated glass building through the winter. From March onwards they can be brought into warmer conditions, 10°C (50°F), to flower from May onwards.

CAMPANULA isophylla 'Alba'

Capsicum

There are several dwarf cultivars of *Capsicum annuum*, commonly called "Peppers" and "Chilli". They are grown in just the same way as the larger fruiting culinary types and tomatoes. Modern cultivars grown for decorative purposes are compact and form attractive fruiting plants in 10-13 cm (4-5 in) pots. They have considerable variation in the shape of fruit and the colour of the leaves. One, called *C. a.* 'Smarty Mixed' has some green and some deep copper-leaved forms and fruits are round or conical, thick or thin and in a very wide range of colour from yellow to red and purple to black.

Once fruit has coloured they are very easy to care for, requiring no more than regular watering. Dryness will cause yellowing of the leaves and leaf fall. Any position is suitable although the leaves will fall quickly if placed in too dark a position. If the leaves do yellow and fall the short stems can be cut and the bright fruits used in dried material arrangements. These annual plants are discarded once the fruits shrivel and lose their attraction.

If you have had trouble with berries falling from the "Christmas Cherry", *Solanum capsicastrum*, and like bright red fruiting plants then give the "Peppers" a try, they are certainly bright and cheerful.

CAPSICUM annuum 'Teno'

Chamaedorea

This small "Parlour Palm" growing eventually to 1 m (3 ft) and usually available as younger, smaller specimens little more than 30 cm (12 in) is an excellent house plant. It is no surprise that palms were popular in the 20's because they are so easy to grow and so resistant to dry and smoky atmospheres as well as quite shady conditions.

Confusion exists over naming with *Chamaedorea elegans* and *Neanthe bella* the most commonly used, although the correct name is *Collinia elegans*. These plants require a minimum winter temperature of 12°C (55°F) and are best in a position which receives indirect light. Keep them just damp through the winter and water regularly during the summer. Sponge the leaves occasionally with water, especially where the plants are in dry atmospheres, as this prevents the leaf tips from going brown. All-peat composts and those growing mediums with a good proportion of peat and leaf mould are ideal.

The occasional liquid feed is advisable during the summer, especially for those plants kept in the smaller sizes of pots, 9-13 cm (3½-5 in) to give root restriction and retain the size of plant. Repotting and potting on is best done in March. The propagation of new plants from seed is best left to the specialist because it demands warm 30°C (85°F) moist conditions. Larger bottle gardens can accomodate *Chamaedorea elegans* where it provides a contrasting leaf form.

CHAMAEDOREA elegans

CHLOROPHYTUM comosum variegatum

Chlorophytum

The common name "Spider Plant" refers to the sprays of young runners produced by mature and larger specimens of *Chlorophytum comosum variegatum*, also known as *C. elatum* 'Variegatum'. Perhaps the more attractive although less descriptive common name "St. Bernard's Lily" is preferable for this excellent house plant which is so easy to grow.

While plants kept on the dry side will survive lower temperature, it is advisable to maintain a minimum winter temperature of 7°C (45°F). In practice the plant grows well at both low and high temperatures. Once again they survive in positions with just a little indirect light but grow best in a position with plenty of light, warmth and regular watering, especially in the summer. Plants which have been allowed to get dry in warm sunny situations have pale transparent looking leaves. Given a good water and feed they quickly recover. All potting composts are suitable including John Innes Potting Compost No. 2 and the proprietary peat composts. Repotting and potting on into a larger size of pot is best done in March and April. New plants are obtained by rooting the young runners produced on the arching stems which also carry insignificant white flowers.

Just the plant for every position from mantels and window ledges to room dividers and even the tops of cupboards.

Chrysanthemum

All too often we take significant cultural advances for granted and the pot *Chrysanthemum* grown to flower the year round is a perfect example. While in some respects the appearance of these flowers out of their natural autumn to Christmas season may distress the purist there is no disputing the long flower life given by year round pot Chrysanthemums. Two cultural factors are used by specialist growers to control flowering, date and ultimate height. The first and most important is day length, once the days start to shorten, as occurs naturally in the autumn, so the light sensitive *Chrysanthemum* forms flower bud. The grower covers his plants with black cloth and black plastic to artificially shorten the day and uses ordinary electric light bulbs to provide extra light when vegetative rather than flower bud forming conditions are required. Second is the use of chemical growth retardents which shorten the flower stem.

It is very difficult for the home gardener to imitate these cultural control factors and the best thing to do is to enjoy the commercially mass produced specimens. When you buy plants look for well developed flowers, if the plants are too tightly in bud, especially in mid winter, they fail to open to their full potential.

A good light position and cool temperature is all that is required. The higher the temperature, over 10°C (50°F) the shorter the life. Keep the plants well watered and do not allow them to wilt if you want to retain the 'shine' on the plants for the longest possible period.

Cissus

CISSUS antartica

Two plants which are very easy to grow and withstand harsh indoor conditions are the "Kangaroo Vine", *Cissus antartica* and the "Grape Ivy", *Rhoicissus rhomboidea*. The latter is more tolerant of widely fluctuating home conditions in which it continues to thrive and grow. Both are excellent green foliage plants producing an abundance of shiny leaves in a short period. They are climbing plants and require canes or support frames, especially for larger specimens. The *Cissus antartica* is self supporting if the growing tip is pinched out regularly to produce short woody growth. One of the most spectacular of all foliage plants is *Cissus discolor*, the young leaves are green and purple with silver inter-veinal marking on the upper surface and deep crimson on the underside. This plant tends to lose its leaves in winter, however, and requires a warm 15°C (60°F) minimum temperature and a moist atmosphere. If you can provide these conditions try growing this plant in a hanging basket where it is most effective.

Most people are better served by the hardier green leaved species, which require a winter temperature of no more than 7°C (45°F) and grow more vigorously at higher temperatures. All potting composts are suitable using the richer ones for the larger specimens grown in 15-20 cm (6-8 in) pots. Less watering is needed in winter, although at steady higher temperatures the plants grow the year round and require regular watering. They survive in very subdued light but to maintain rich green colour and sturdy growth it is advisable to site the plants in a light position every now and then, especially in winter, to allow recovery from soft elongated growth which occurs in warm dark conditions. New plants are produced from cuttings.

Larger plants of the green leaved types make excellent specimens to stand on the floor in the corners of rooms and against room dividers.

CISSUS striata

Foliage of CISSUS : 1. antartica, 2. striata, 3. capensis, 4. discolor, 5. Rhoicissus rhomboidea

CLERODENDRUM *thomsonae*

Clerodendrum

A really startling June to September flowering climber is the *Clerodendrum thomsonae*. Perhaps not the ideal house plant, from the point of view of winter appearance and somewhat demanding cultural requirement, but see it in flower and you will agree it is well worth the extra effort.

It requires a minimum winter temperature of 13°C (55°F) and a light situation, lightly shaded from hot sun in mid summer when temperatures of 18°C (65°F) are the ideal. Restrict watering through the winter to keep the plant just ticking over and then water freely in spring and summer when growth is rapid. Given adequate root room, 15-20 cm (6-8 in) pots, specimens over 2 m (6 ft) high can be grown, smaller plants can be produced with the root restriction of smaller pots. Any repotting is best done in April and new plants are produced from cuttings in spring rooted under very warm conditions.

CLEYERA *japonica tricolor*

Cleyera

This evergreen shrub with shiny foliage, described by some people as similar to *Camellia* in texture, is tender although surviving outside in frost free areas. Some confusion exists over naming and *Cleyera japonica tricolor* is also known as *C. ochnacea.* and *Eurya japonica.* Under garden conditions it forms a densely leaved plant up to 2 m (6 ft) high.

Small plants with roots restricted by the use of smaller 9-13 cm (3½-5 in) pots make excellent house plants and are ideal for window sill and reasonably well lit positions. Quite low winter temperatures, 5°C (40°F) are acceptable for this almost hardy perennial which grows well in John Innes Potting Compost No. 1 and similar soil based composts. Propagation is by cuttings taken in spring.

A bowl of mixed house plants including:- Ficus benjamina (top) Ficus elastica 'Tricolor' (top right) Codiaeum variegatum (centre) X Fatshedera lizei (centre) Acorus gramineus variegatus (left side) Maranta leuconeura (left side) Ficus pumila (right side) Pellionia daveauana (right foreground) Neoregelia carolinae (centre foreground) Scindapsus aureus (front trailing) Begonia Hybrid in flower.

Clivia

CLIVIA miniata

An accommodating plant, *Clivia miniata* thrives in most situations. Dark green, strap-like leaves are carried the year round and the bold orange or red flower heads on thick stems, 42-45 cm (15-18 in) high, appear from March to August. If the plants are to flower every year keep them on the dry side through the winter and on a frost free sunny window sill. Out of flower the leaves are not particularly interesting but careful siting and treatment at this time is necessary to secure the flowers.

Early spring sees the need to increase the watering and provide a temperature of 16°C (61°F). Large, very root bound specimens can be divided up and the strong side shoots potted up singly in February, using John Innes Potting Compost No. 2 or something similar. Do not be in a hurry to either move on into larger pots or to divide up because these plants grow happily with some root restriction. When dividing up plants be careful not to damage the rather brittle succulent roots. Young plants can also be raised from seed.

Commonly called "Kaffir Lily", the large flowering plants make eye-catching specimens but I prefer to see smaller plants used in groups with other indoor foliage plants.

Codiaeum

Brilliant and changing leaf colour is the feature of *Codiaeum variegatum pictum* and its various cultivars. Better known to most of us by the common name "Croton" this plant has found a new lease of life in the home with the steady even temperature provided by modern central heating. While the best growth occurs with a steady even temperature of 15°C (60°F), plants will survive at lower levels down to 13°C

CODIAEUM variegatum 'Philip Geduldig'

(55°F). The important point is to avoid wildly fluctuating temperatures and cold draughts which will cause sudden leaf drop. A test of your cultural skill, and a test of the professional gardeners of yesteryear, is to grow large specimens 1-2 m (3-6 ft) high and retain the lower leaves.

The tricky period for leaf retention is mid winter, be sure to reduce watering at this time and keep the plants in a light if not sunny window, bright light improving the leaf colour as well as growth. Once they have settled down in house conditions they will give great pleasure for a considerable period of time and early summer is a good time to start the period of acclimatisation to room conditions. The very narrow leaved forms are usually easier although less colourful plants.

March and April is the best time to move to larger pots and repot using compost of John Innes potting compost No. 2 strength. Wipe the leaves regularly with a damp cloth as this not only improves the appearance but keeps down red spider mite under hot dry room conditions. Ideally syringe the plants occasionally through the summer when a dilute liquid feed once a fortnight improves established specimens.

Where plants have either become leggy or outgrown the space available for them they can be pruned back in March and, under warm moist conditions, new growth will soon be made. Cover the cut surface with powered charcoal (crumble up some burnt matches for this) to prevent loss of white sap.

Coleus

An indication of the tremendous range and variety of leaf colour provided by *Coleus blumei* can be seen from the illustrations. One could well call them the poor man's "Croton" for they are cheap, easy to grow and very colourful. The thin insignificant flower spikes should be pinched out as soon as they appear because although of succulent and shrubby perennial growth, when *Coleus* flowers and sets seed it reduces the production of colourful young leaves.

While named cultivars, with particularly attractive leaf markings, can be overwintered and new stock propagated from cuttings taken from such plants in spring, the improvement in seed raised stocks has encouraged the raising of new plants each year from seed sown from January to March. All plants grow best at a temperature of 15°C (60°F) although woody plants will overwinter at 10°C (50°F). They grow well in all composts especially the proprietary all peat formulations.

A good light position is needed to obtain well balanced growth but in strong sunlight in mid summer the leaf colour fades. In addition to the bold leaf forms illustrated, recent strains also have smaller frilled leaves and some have puckered leaf edges. When treated as annuals 9-13 cm (3½-5 in) pots are sufficient.

COLUMNEA gloriosa

Columnea

One of the brightest and most eye-catching trailing plants, *Columnea gloriosa*, requires the right indoor conditions for success in producing the 0.6-1.3 m (2-4 ft) hanging branches spurting out the scarlet flowers from October to April. It really is a hanging plant and must be placed in a container which allows the trailing branches to develop unhindered. The darker leaved cultivar is *C. g.* 'Purpurea', smaller leaves and even longer branches are the features of *C. microphylla*.

While plants will survive in the dry atmosphere of centrally heated homes a warm moist atmosphere is needed to encourage flowering. Hence flowering plants must be used either as dispensable after flowering or moved to the greenhouse or conservatory, warm, 13-15°C (55-60°F), moist atmosphere to grow through the summer and develop sufficiently to produce next season's flowers. The all-peat and peat enriched composts are ideal for these plants which need keeping just nicely moist the year round. See that they are in a light position through the winter and in indirect light through the summer.

A high temperature is needed to root the cuttings in late spring and any repotting or potting on is best done in June. The *Columnea* is an excellent plant for plastic hanging baskets with drip catching saucers and the very popular string and rope supported plant containers.

Cordyline

CORDYLINE stricta

Confusion exists over the naming of *Cordyline* and *Dracaena*, both genera containing attractive foliage plants well suited to indoor decoration. They all develop a central stem and in time produce specimens 1 m and more in height. One of the most popular house plants is *Cordyline terminalis*, with bold palm-like leaves growing ultimately ½-1 m (18 in-3 ft) high, and two cultivars, *C. t.* 'Prince Albert' and *C. t.* 'Atom' are recommended. Leaf colouring of the different forms varies from green to dark purple and some have cream variegation. Much taller ultimately are *C. stricta* with slender upright form reaching 2 m (6 ft) high and *C. rubra* 'Bruantii', which reaches 3 m (9 ft) or more.

All plants grow well in the all-peat and peat enriched potting composts and specimens are best repotted once every 2-3 years in March. Large specimens will require a 16-20 cm (-8 in) pot and all *Cordyline* and *Dracaena* require a minimum winter temperature of 13°C (55°F). Reduce the moisture level of the compost but maintain regularity in watering through the winter, when *Cordyline* is best in a light sunny position. They are best out of direct sunlight during the summer.

The rather woody, eventually shrubby sort of growth makes the *Cordyline* an easy house plant once established in the home. Good, large plants make excellent specimens especially when stood on the floor to be viewed from above. They also thrive in groups of other subjects arranged in self-watering containers, which are used increasingly in the home and office. In my experience the best time to introduce these plants in to the home is early summer. Once a feel is obtained for their water requirement they give a long decorative life.

New plants are propagated in May/June from the tip and sections of stem from older plants which have become bare at the base. Very warm, humid conditions are required to root these cuttings. The recently introduced *Dracaena marginata tricolor* is a very attractive house plant.

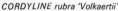

CORDYLINE rubra 'Bruantii'

CORDYLINE rubra 'Volkaertii'

DRACAENA marginata tricolor

CORDYLINE terminalis

39

CROSSANDRA infudibuliformis

Crossandra

The *Crossandra infundibuliformis*, also known as *C. undulaefolia*, is a pot plant with very long lasting flowers. The spikes of flowers up to 10 cm (4 in) long appear from April right through to the autumn.

They are not the easiest of plants to keep through the winter and require a light, warm and humid atmosphere. A minimum winter temperature of 13°C (55°F) is required and in many homes it is best to treat this plant as an expendable subject after flowering.

Very young plants will flower and for indoor decoration specimens in 9-13 cm (3½-5 in) pots are sufficient and either the all-peat composts or soil based composts to John Innes No. 2 strength are suitable. The compost should be just moist when plants are kept indoors overwinter, increasing the watering when growth commences in the spring. Light shade is needed from direct hot sun in summer and a liquid feed once a week through the summer.

A selection of the Cyclamen persicum hybrids currently available

43

CYRTOMIUM falcatum 'Rochfordianum'

Cyrtomium

One of the easiest ferns to grow indoors, the "Japanese Holly Fern", sometimes referred to as "Hollies", is listed under the latin names *Cyrtomium falcatum* and *Polystichum falcatum*. The rich dark green fronds are shiny, they look as if they have been polished, and survive quite severe indoor conditions including poor light, comparatively dry atmospheres and cool temperatures. The cultivar *C.f.* 'Rochfordianum' is recommended for its very much larger fronds, reaching some 30-45 cm (12-18 in) in height and spread.

A minimum winter temperature of 7°C (45°F) is required and like all ferns the *Cyrtomium* grows well in the all-peat composts. Small plants provide a contrasting foliage shape and colour in bowl arrangements of mixed plants. They also look well in association with spring flowering bulbs. Young specimens in 9 cm (3½ in) pots are ideal for the average home and larger specimens 2-3 years old will require a 13-15 cm (5-6 in) diameter pot. Large plants can be divided in April, which is the best time for repotting.

Be sure to keep plants well watered and shaded from hot sun through the summer months when a fortnightly liquid feed is also advisable.

CYTISUS x racemosus

Cytisus

This tender plant will reach 2 m (6 ft) in height and spread under the right garden conditions and is commonly called "Genista". Given some root restraint by pot culture and the trimming back of branches, *Cytisus x racemosus* makes an attractive, fragrant spring flowering house plant. It grows well in soil based compost, for example John Innes No. 2 and the 13 cm (5 in) size pot. A minimum winter temperature of 7°C (45°F) is required, the plants being brought into warmer temperatures 10°C (50°F) plus in early spring to produce flowers from February to April.

After flowering, continue watering and give a dilute liquid feed every 14 days. Once the chance of frost has passed these plants can be stood outside and plunged in garden soil through the summer but be sure to see that they are kept well watered. October is a good time to repot established specimens and pot on young plants produced from cuttings rooted in July.

All the flowering shoots should be trimmed off after flowering, this retains shape, keeps the plants compact and ensures the production of new shoots which will carry next year's flowers.

Dieffenbachia

Warm and humid conditions are provided in tropical America, the home of *Dieffenbachia* and we need to imitate this in the home to some extent for the best results. Once established in the home they will settle down to drier conditions but the warmth is fundamental to satisfactory growth. Several different forms of *Dieffenbachia picta* are the most commonly offered today, with *D.p.* 'Exotica Perfection' which has basal sideshoots and the large leaved *D.p.* 'Tropic Snow' recommended.

They have the local common name "Leopard Lily" in their native West Indies but there is the more widely used common name "Dumb Cane" as it is said that if the sap gets anywhere near the mouth the tongue swells up and prevents speech. If you should therefore be taking a cutting or removing leaves, we suggest you wash your hands thoroughly after handling a cut surface and avoid getting the sap near the mouth and eyes. The leaves are most attractive and as a result this plant is a popular one to use in the home and office, both as a specimen and in association with other plants in larger groups. It will eventually grow 0.6-1.3 m (2-4 ft) in height.

Richer soil based composts to John Innes No. 3 strength are ideal and a 13-15 cm (5-6 in) pot is needed. Repotting is best done in April and May with the largest specimens being moved on into tubs up to 30 cm (12 in) diameter. Place in a light position through the winter but out of direct sunshine in the summer. Given the ideal 16-18°C (61-65°F) temperature, *Dieffenbachia* will continue to grow the year round. They will, however, survive lower temperatures even down to 10°C (50°F) for a short period but this may result in the loss of the bottom leaves. Given lower winter temperatures, the watering should be reduced. A monthly liquid feed through the summer will improve speed of growth and leaf size.

Cuttings made from the tip of the plant and sections of the stem are rooted in early summer but a very humid and warm, 21°C (70°F) atmosphere and rooting medium is needed.

DIEFFENBACHIA amoena

DIEFFENBACHIA picta 'Exotica'

Dipladenia

Beautiful rich evergreen foliage and bright pink flowers on young wood are the qualities provided by *Dipladenia splendens*. Where plants are allowed to develop freely, growing in the greenhouse border soil, they are twining and climbing plants which grow to 5 cm (15 ft). Young plants, no more than 20 cm (8 in) high, will flower freely however and either small plants in 9 cm (3½-in) pots or larger specimens with wire and cane support make attractive indoor subjects. There is a white flowered form *D. boliviensis* with larger flowers and leaves.

During the winter months keep the compost dry, almost to the point where the plant wilts, and a minimum temperature of 13°C (55°F). When the temperature rises in spring to 15°C (60°F) growth speeds up and the plants need watering freely and the occasional sponging of the leaves with a damp cloth. Continue this level of watering until the flowering finishes in October. Both species require warmth and humidity to succeed. A dilute liquid feed every 10-14 days through the summer improves growth.

The all-peat and soil based composts are suitable and repotting is best done in spring. Any pruning should be carried out after flowering when indoor plants, which have to be kept small, should be cut back hard retaining no more than 5-10 cm (2-4 in) of the current year's growth. Larger specimens may be left unpruned to provide the twining growth.

DIPLADENIA splendens

DIZYGOTHECA elegantissima

Dizygotheca

This tender shrub or small tree from Australia has very attractive, slender leaflets which account for the common name "Spider Plant". The correct name is *Dizygotheca elegantissima*, although it is also known as *Aralia elegantissima*. Growing eventually to 1.6 m (5 ft) in height, the leaves on young plants open a deep copper and change to dark green as they age.

The stem may be woody but this plant is far from hard and requires careful cultivation for satisfactory growth. A minimum winter temperature of 13°C (55°f) is required and ideally a warmer, humid atmosphere. Moisture in the atmosphere reduces the damage from Red Spider attack and syringing the leaves with water, especially during the higher temperature periods in summer, is an advantage. Choose a light position, ideally out of direct sun in high summer and pot into either the all-peat or soil based composts in May. Plants in 9-13 cm (3½-5 in) pots are ideal for most home uses although larger specimens to 1 m (3 ft) or more can be grown in 20-25 cm (8-10 in) pots.

Little pruning is necessary except where cold temperatures and overwatering have caused leaf fall and thin, bare plants. Such specimens can be rejuvenated by cutting hard back in March when new young growth will be made from the stump.

DRACAENA fragrans 'Massangeana'

DRACAENA sanderiana

Dracaena

Tender, evergreen, commonly called "Dragon Plants", the long narrow leaved forms of *Dracaena* are the most popular. Good examples are *D. deremensis* 'Warneckii', dark green with central grey strip and longitudinal white lines as a demarkation between the grey and green leaf edges. *D.d.* 'Bansei' is a more delicate form with dark green leaves and central white stripe which requires warmer and more humid conditions than *D.d.* 'Warneckii'. *D. fragrans* 'Lindenii', *D. fragrans* 'Massangcana' and *D. sanderiana*. Quite different in leaf shape is *D. godseffiana* with rounded laurel-like leaves, green spotted white and carried on thin, wiry stems.

The last two mentioned species will take a lower winter minimum temperature of 10°C (55°F) and the drier atmosphere of the average home, while the remainder require 15°C (60°F) and more humid conditions for satisfactory growth. A light position is needed to get the strongest variation in leaf colour. Watering should be reduced in autumn and again in spring, increasing during the summer months when a liquid feed once every fourteen days encourages strong growth.

DRACAENA fragrans 'Lindenii'

Dracaena

Both the soil based and the all-peat composts give excellent growth and 9-13 cm (3½-5 in) pots are sufficient for the size of plant grown in most homes. Taller specimens of *D. sanderiana* grow upright, take up little room which makes this plant acceptable as a larger plant to decorate the corner of a small room.

New plants are produced from tip cuttings and pieces of stem 8 cm (3 in) in length, the stem pieces produce shoots which initially are green but the true colour is produced as soon as the cuttings become established.

A hot, 21-24°C (70-75°F), humid atmosphere and rooting medium is needed to root cuttings.

The younger smaller plants of *D. sanderiana* are very attractive in mixed arrangements of house plants, for example in bowls, dishes and troughs. The upright linear foliage and striking white stripes contrast with softer and more rounded green leaved subjects. The cultivars *D.f.* 'Lindenii' and *D.f.* 'Massangeana' are popular as larger specimens and *D. sanderiana* as smaller specimens due to its more compact habit and shorter leaves.

Erica

There are two "Heathers" which are not sufficiently hardy for garden use but make colourful winter flowering indoor pot plants, namely *Erica gracilis* with pink and white or purple flowers and the white flowering form sometimes called *E. nivalis,* and *Erica hyemalis* with pink flowers. These plants are usually sold in flower from September to Christmas and into the new year. Commercially produced plants are usually in small pots with very restricted root growth and care must be taken to see that they do not dry out.

The purple flowered forms sold during September and October may be used outdoors in sheltered positions to give a fine display of colour up to December provided there are no severe frosts. They are used for outdoor bedding in Europe, particularly in German gardens, parks and cemeteries.

Lime free compost and water is needed for the heathers and either all-peat or peat-sand composts are excellent. A cool atmosphere is needed with a minimum winter temperature of 5°C (41°F) Avoid temperatures over 15°C (60°F) and be sure the compost is kept damp at all times. Feeding is not necessary. The commercially produced flowering specimens are best considered expendable, if you do wish to keep them for a second season repot into a size larger container in March. New plants can be obtained by taking short cuttings at the same time. It is advisable to keep established plants outside from early summer until September, plunging the pots in either soil or damp peat to retain moisture and help reduce the chance of the compost drying out. Shading from sun will not be necessary except in exceptionally hot sunny conditions.

Foreground *Euphorbia pulcherrima 'Mikkelrochford Red'* with *Sansevieria trifasciata 'Laurentii'* and *Hedera canariensis 'Variegata'*.

Euphorbia

One of the most startlingly coloured plants is *Euphorbia pulcherrima*, commonly called and very well known as "Poinsettia". Whilst there are pink and white forms, and cultural systems which provide flowering plants the year round, scarlet cultivars for Christmas remain the most popular. The bright colours come from bracts surrounding the cluster of yellow flowers at the tip of each shoot. These bracts provide up to five months of colour in the home. Grown out of doors in sub tropical areas, *E. pulcherrima* is a shrub reaching 1½-2 m high but growers keep young plants in pots short by pinching and applying growth retarding chemicals. Specially selected froms like *E.p.* 'Mikkelrochford Red' are suited for indoor use because of the compact, free branching growth and very large colourful bracts. This has been followed by the more brilliantly coloured form 'Mikkel Improved Rochford' and an outstanding dark pink sport called 'Mikkel Rochford Fantastic'.

Quite different in form *E. fulgens* produces arching branches which, during the winter months, carry bunches of small flowers at each leaf joint.

Both plants require a minimum temperature of 13°C (55°F) and a light position through the winter.

All these plants require watering through the winter, just kept nicely damp, *not* overwatered. The occasional liquid feed is beneficial especially if growing for a second year in the same pot. They can be repotted at the start of a new growing season in proprietary peat composts.

E. pulcherrima

50

X FATSHEDERA lizei

X Fatshedera

One of the few plants which have come to us as a result of two genera, in this case *Fatsia* and *Hedera*, being cross pollinated and the resultant seedling forming a new plant *X Fatshedera*. While this plant is a hardy outdoor shrub it is widely grown as a very attractive indoor foliage plant. In addition to the very attractive bright green leaved *X Fatshedera lizei* there is the form with a creamy white variegation to the leaves called *X Fatshedera lizei* 'Variegata'.

The perfect foliage plant for indoors where the temperatures are cool and may even drop below 4°C (40°F). If the plants become too tall and outgrow their pot they can be pruned back and moved to a larger pot in March and April. Any general potting compost is suitable and the occasional liquid feed during the summer will increase the speed of growth and size of leaves. They will thrive in both light and more shaded positions indoors, although in very dark positions the plants will in time become drawn.

Fatsia
syn. Aralia

FATSIA japonica 'Variegata'

Popular because of its easy nature is *Fatsia japonica*, also called *Aralia japonica* and *Aralia sieboldii* and commonly erroneously called "Castor Oil Plant". This plant is hardy in areas which avoid very severe frost and is grown in gardens for both evergreen foliage and its white flower clusters in autumn and early winter. Indoors it is used purely for the large, shiny rich green leaves. Very easy to grow, the Fatsia will stand darker, shaded positions and temperatures indoors which could fall below -1°C (30°F). Repotting in any potting compost is best done in March and April. Any cutting back to retain size is also best done at this time.

The larger plants form attractive specimens at a modest price. While *F. japonica*, the green leaved species, can be raised from seed the creamy white variegated *F.j. variegata* must be raised vegetatively.

The Fatsia is an excellent plant to grow as a specimen in a large container in halls, which tend to be shaded, and in sun lounges and porches where low temperatures occur. If your plant has become too large for the window sill, why not move it out on to the patio or terrace?

Ficus

The hardiest species are the "Mistletoe Fig", *Ficus diversifolia*, a rather sparse leaved plant with berries carried throughout the year and the "Creeping Fig", *Ficus pumila*. Both survive a minimum winter temperature of 7°C (45°F) and quite dark, shaded positions. There are a great many uses for *Ficus pumila* grown in 9 cm (3½ in) pots to trail over the sides of plant troughs, to grow up and over wall brackets, to furnish the front of mixed bowls of plants, and it is especially useful in bottle gardens and terrariums.

Ideally a higher minimum winter temperature of 16°C (60°F) is needed for the green leaved *Ficus radicans* and even better *F.r.* 'Variegata', the "Variegated Trailing Fig", which can be used in all the roles listed for the creeping fig. The higher temperature is also needed for; the "Weeping Fig", *Ficus benjamina*, a charming plant with most attractive form; the range of *Ficus elastica* cultivars; and the "Fiddle Leaf Fig", *Ficus lyrata*, which has really large leaves like elephants' ears, a plant which needs plenty of space to develop and be seen at its best.

If you wish to keep these less hardy forms at lower winter temperatures be sure to reduce the winter watering carefully.

The "India-rubber Plant", or just plain "Rubber Plant", is so popular mention must be made of the various forms currently available. All types have developed from the green leaved *Ficus elastica* and more recently the green plants sold commercially are of the variety *F.e. decora* and the "Improved Rubber Plant" *F.e.* 'Robusta'. The last two have more compact growth, larger darker green leaves, very attractive red sheath to the growing tip and are easier to grow.

There are also several variegated forms with the leaves blotched and spotted white, cream and yellow over green. The better forms, including *F.e.* 'Doescheri' and *F.e.* 'Tricolor', have the younger leaves flushed pink. It should be remembered that the variegated forms are more demanding in regard to the position (in good light but out of direct sun in high summer), temperature and watering.

THE VARIOUS FORMS OF FICUS: **1.** *F. elastica 'Schryveriana'* **2.** *F. radicans 'Variegata'* **3.** *F. lyrata* **4.** *F. triangularis* **5.** *F. elastica 'Doescheri'* **6.** *F. benjamina* **7.** *F. radicans* **9.** *F. elastica decora.*

FICUS elastica decora

FICUS pumila

They all grow well in the proprietary peat composts as well as in the soil based mixes like John Innes No. 2 potting compost. Any repotting and potting on is best done in spring, April is a good month. This repotting should only be necessary once every two years and it is better to keep the roots restricted than move to too large a pot.

Where plants are in an excessively large pot watering becomes much more difficult.

A good guide to pot size for *Ficus elastica* is, a 13 cm (5 in) pot for plants up to 90 cm (2½ ft), 15 cm (6 in) pot — 1.5 m (4½ ft) and 20 cm (8 in) pot — 2 m (6 ft).

FICUS elastica tricolor

FICUS benjamina

FICUS diversifolia

A decorative bowl containing: Codiaeum variegatum, Dizygotheca elegantissima, Gynura sarmentosa, Vriesia (almost hidden), Pellionia daveauana, Peperomia caperata 'Variegata', Ficus pumila.

A Fuchsia trained on a single stem to form a standard

Fuchsia

Some of the most adaptable and versatile of all summer flowering plants are the *Fuchsia* hybrids, flowering from May to October. The varieties of weeping and pendulous habit can be used in hanging baskets and to the front of plant troughs.

They will not stand hard frost and need a minimum winter temperature of 5°C (40°F.) From October to early spring it is a matter of keeping these deciduous plants alive with the compost just damp and the cool temperature held steady. Early in spring increase the temperature to 13-15°C (55-60°F) and with the development of new young growth increase the watering and feed every 10-14 days.

When flowering plants are purchased in spring and summer be sure to place in a light position and keep well watered. A check in growth caused by dryness and lack of light results in flower bud drop. If this does happen keep the plant in a light position and water as necessary because new growth will soon be made and flowering will quickly follow.

All composts are suitable, especially the loam based John Innes No. 2 potting compost. Large plants quickly exhaust the food in the compost and liquid feeding will then be necessary.

New plants are obtained by taking cuttings 5-8 cm (2-3 in) long from the young growth in spring and summer. They root very easily in early summer, even in a glass of water.

Tall and straggly plants can be rejuvenated by pruning hard back in spring.

Gesneria

The brilliant scarlet flowers of *Gesneria cardinalis,* also known as *G. macrantha,* are produced from early summer to mid autumn. These tuberous rooted plants require treatment similar to *Begonia* and *Gloxinia.* They thrive in the all-peat composts and require a warm moist atmosphere for the best results.

Most home owners wisely treat the *Gesneria* as a source of bright summer flower colour and then discard. Being modestly priced it is cheaper to replace each year rather than trouble to provide the 12°C (55°F) in winter and 15°C (65°F) in early spring when the plants are started into new growth.

While these plants require a light position, it should be indirect light and away from direct strong sunshine. The compost should be kept nicely moist through spring and summer. If plants have been dried off after flowering and the tubers kept frost free through the winter, they should be repotted in spring, the tubers just covered with compost. Commercial plants are usually raised from seed sown in very warm, damp conditions in January. The strain *Gesneria macrantha* 'Compacta' is widely used because of the neat compact growth and free flowering habit.

GESNERIA cardinalis

GREVILLEA robusta

Grevillea

Australia gives us the feathery, light green foliage of *Grevillea robusta,* commonly called the "Silk Oak". It is easy to grow, eventually reaching 2 m (6 ft) high with a spread of 0.6 m (2 ft). Small seedlings in 9-13 cm (3½-5 in) pots grow well in the home and are best in a light position. Cool conditions are ideal with a minimum winter temperature of 7°C (45°F). All composts are suitable and John Innes Potting Compost No. 2 is ideal.

Keep the plants well watered during the summer when growth is rapid, dry compost causes yellowing of the leaves and premature leaf fall. If this does happen and the plant becomes bare at the base, it can be cut back to encourage new shoots to come from lower down the stem. Young plants well furnished with foliage to the base of the stem are by far the most attractive, however, and if plants have been allowed to get dry it is better to replace with new young plants or, alternatively, raise new plants from seed sown in March in a temperature of 15°C (60°F).

Larger specimens of this plant are used in the garden for summer bedding display and if your plant outgrows the room available for it then start again with another young plant indoors and use the large plant for a summer on the patio or in the garden.

GUZMANIA lingulata

Guzmania

Another member of the Bromeliad "Pineapple", family is *Guzmania lingulata*. It has startling scarlet flower bracts which remain an attraction for weeks even if the small yellow flowers in the centre are short lived. The leaves are up to 0.5 m (18 in) long and the flower spike 0.3 m (12 in) high.

Similar in leaf form but with an even more striking bract and flowers is *G. monostachya*. The bract can be thick columnar stem some 8-10" high with a domed head red in colour with dark brown to black linear markings and white flowers. These plants need a very light, airy compost, free of lime, the all peat ones are suitable especially if the peat is coarse. Water freely in summer and keep just moist in winter, using lime-free water, for example rain water. A shaded position, out of direct strong sunshine, is required. Humid conditions are best and a steady temperature the year round of 16°C (60°F) is recommended for *Guzmania*. New plants are obtained by cutting off rooted off-sets from the parent plant in April.

GYNURA sarmentosa

Gynura

Masses of rich purple hairs on the dark green stems and leaves of *Gynura* give an appearance of the pile on velvet. There are two species grown indoors, *G. aurantiaca* and *G. sarmentosa*, the latter having a more trailing habit. Both are most attractive as young plants and once two years old are best replaced with new young plants. Orange "Groundsel" shaped flowers appear from February onwards, these are best removed because the colour clashes and the flowers have an unpleasant smell.

All the potting composts are suitable and kinds of John Innes No. 2 Potting Compost strength are ideal. While lower temperatures are survived, a minimum winter temperature of 13°C (55°F) is recommended. Place in a light window and keep just damp through the winter. They will need more water through the summer when a position away from direct sunlight is advisable.

Hedera

One of the easiest of all evergreen plants to grow indoors and out in a fantastically diverse range of situations is *Hedera*, "Ivy". Most popular is the large, white and silver over green leaved *Hedera canariensis* 'Variegata', also known as *H.c.* 'Gloire de Marengo', the variegated form of the "Canary Island Ivy". The "Common Ivy", *Hedera helix*, has smaller leaves and is the source of countless cultivars of widely varying leaf shape and colour. From the most aptly named *H.h.* 'Glacier' which has small leaves so attractively 'frosted' white and silver over green it looks like ice, to *H.h.* 'Goldheart' with neat growth and a bold deep yellow centre to the dark green leaves.

While the variegated "Canary Island Ivy" is said to be less hardy, all the house plant cultivars have survived outside through the average British winter and withstand quite severe frost. Soft, rapidly growing young plants from warm glasshouse conditions will be damaged by frost and wind, however, and a gradual hardening off is necessary before leaving indoor plants outside unprotected.

The sight of the "Common Ivy" growing in hedge bottoms, up trees, on walls in polluted city atmospheres clearly indicates the tenacity with which the house plant ivies will cling to life. They thrive in all room positions although the variegated leaf forms lose their colour and tend to go green in very dark situations. Specimens indoors will survive in unheated rooms although the best results will be obtained with plants in temperatures from 10-15°C (50-60°F) and bright diffused light.

Hot, dry conditions encourage attack by red spider mite, identified by the leaves taking on a dull, rusty appearance. An occasional syringing with water and wiping of the leaves with a damp cloth reduces the chance of red spider multiplication and improves the appearance of the leaves. All composts are suitable, with the larger specimens in 15-20 cm (6-8 in) pots requiring those composts with higher fertiliser levels. Fortnightly liquid feeds through spring, summer and early autumn increase the speed of growth.

New plants are obtained by rooting cuttings, and older plants which have lost leaves from the base can be rejuvenated by pruning hard back in spring when new growth will come from bare stems. Perfect plants to drift over the edge of every kind of container. One of the best indoor climbers and plants for hanging containers where growth can climb up the supports and trail over the sides.

HEDERA helix 'Marmorata'

HEDERA canariensis 'Variegata'

HEDERA helix 'Green Ripple'

HEDERA helix 'Chicago'

HEDERA helix 'Sagittaefolia'

59

Hibiscus

This sub tropical tender shrub growing to 4 m (12 ft) in height and spread in the open ground can also be used as an eye-catching indoor flowering pot plant. The very large colourful flowers are produced from every leaf joint on quite young specimens from June to September. The flowers are not long lasting, the single flowers having an approximate life of 24 hours, but so many are produced in a season and so frequently the plant is almost always in flower.

Flowering plants in 9-13 cm (3½-5 in) pots, sold in shops and garden centres are young rooted cuttings kept compact by pinching and the use of growth retardants. If these plants are to be kept indoors for several years and not treated as a one-summer supply of colour it is necessary to restrict root growth by keeping in the smaller flower pot sizes and pruning back hard in spring. This pruning consists of cutting all young growth back to within 7 cm (3 in) of the old wood.

There are both double and single flowering hybrids in shades of red, pink and yellow. The variety *H. rosa-sinensis* 'Cooperi' has smaller crimson flowers but the leaves are dark green, attractively variegated white, pink and red. Given a winter temperature of 15°C (60°F) the *Hibiscus* retains its leaves through the winter but at lower temperatures, 7°C (45°F), the leaves fall in the winter and the plants require less water, keeping the compost just damp.

Both soil based John Innes and the proprietary peat composts are suitable, with repotting best done in March and April. They require a light position shaded from direct sun in mid-summer when the compost must be kept moist.

If you have plants which are outgrowing the room available for them try using for one last summer outside for patio decoration. The *Hibiscus* are accommodating indoor plants, they respond to the secateurs.

Hibiscus rosa-sinensis, a double hybrid

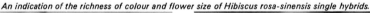

An indication of the richness of colour and flower size of Hibiscus rosa-sinensis single hybrids.

Hoya

There are several unusual features about *Hoya*, commonly called "Wax Flower" and the first is their exquisite wax-like, white petalled, star-shaped flowers. Warm, 15°C (60°F), moist conditions are needed to encourage flowering on the bushy *Hoya bella*, growing to 0.3 m (18 in) in height and spread, and the trailing *Hoya carnosa* which has the unusual habit of producing a whole bare stem of growth before the leaves form.

One of the two variegated leaf forms of *Hoya carnosa* should be chosen for normal home conditions. The thick evergreen leaves are very attractive in their own right and will only require a minimum winter temperature of 10°C (50°F), surviving at 7°C (45°F). All the *Hoya* types grow well in the peat composts and while *Hoya bella* is excellent in hanging baskets, *Hoya carnosa* is best either climbing up supports in the conservatory or kept in smaller pots, both growing naturally and twining.

These plants are best left unpruned except perhaps for pinching out the tips of young growth to encourage branching. Keep the plants on the dry side through the winter, especially if kept at the lower temperatures. Watering can be increased as the days lengthen, the weather becomes warmer and speed of growth increases. A dilute liquid feed once every three to four weeks will improve growth and the provision of a humid atmosphere encourages flower bud formation. Do not cut off flowers as they fade as additional flowers are often produced from the old flower stalks.

HOYA carnosa 'Variegata'

HOWEA forsteriana

Howea

A very popular palm, regaining popularity with the return to fashion of victoriana, *Howea forsteriana* is also called *Kentia*. Mature specimens will reach 3 m (9 ft high and 2 m (6 ft) spread but younger plants in 13-15 cm (5-6 in) pots are the most widely used indoors. The less common *H. belmoreana* has finer more delicate leaflets, is slower growing and requires greater warmth than the tougher *H. forsteriana*.

The last mentioned is a very easy indoor plant, growing well in the soil based and proprietary peat composts. Place in a light position through the winter but out of direct sun in mid-summer. Restrict the watering in the winter to keep just moist and maintain a minimum temperature of 10°C (50°F). *H. forsteriana* will survive a temperature as low as 7°C (45°F). *H. belmoreana*, however, requires a minimum temperature of 15°C (60°F). In summer, with increasing temperatures and more rapid growth, keep the pots well watered and give large plants a fortnightly liquid feed.

Repotting is best done every two years after plants have fully filled a 13 cm (5 in) pot. New plants are raised from seed, a job best left to the professional grower because a high propagating bed temperature, 27°C (80°F), is required.

The only pruning is the removal of dead leaves, and the occasional sponging of the leaves and syringing with water helps deter red spider attack. Should the tips of the leaves turn brown they may be trimmed with scissors.

Hydrangea

HYDRANGEA *macrophylla blue hybrid*

HYDRANGEA *macrophylla pink hybrid*

The *Hydrangea macrophylla* cultivars are very accommodating plants because if you let them get dry the leaves and flowers quickly wilt and recover equally quickly, given a good watering. Plants for indoor decoration are started into growth by gently forcing early in the New Year. Bringing a series of plants into the warmer conditions, 13°C (55°F), at weekly intervals from early January provides a succession of flower from April to June. There is a new "Lacecap Hydrangea", *H.m.* 'Libella' which makes a spectacular pot plant, the ring of white flowers surround the centre sterile head which is usually 'blued'.

These plants require a lime-free soil, especially the blue-flowered cultivars which revert to pink if lime and chalk are present. The rich blue colour is obtained by keeping certain pink cultivars in acid soil and treating with Aluminium sulphate. Shops sell Hydrangea colourant for this. Both John Innes and the proprietary peat composts are suitable as long as the lime in the compost has been reduced. The pink and white cultivars do not change colour in the presence of lime.

After flowering you can cut hard back and either plant in a sheltered spot in the garden or repot and leave out of doors to produce new growth before bringing in from the frost in the autumn and repeating the forcing treatment.

During the flowering period these plants can be in very light and quite shaded positions. A good, light position is needed from the start of growth in spring to the flowering stage. Regular liquid feeding is needed during periods of new leaf and flower development.

Hypocyrta

The wax-like orange flower of *Hypocyrta glabra* emerging from a pronounced green calyx clearly explains the common names "Clog Plant" and, when you look at the fish-like opening of the flower, "Goldfish Plant". For my money the true value of this plant, however, is the thick, glossy dark green leaves. Although related to the *Columnea*, the *Hypocyrta* will survive quite low winter temperatures, 10°C (50°F) if the compost is kept just damp.

They grow very well in the proprietary peat composts and can also be grown in the soil based ones. Young plants will need 9 cm (3½ in) pots and larger specimens are attractive in hanging baskets. Positions in full sun are acceptable and the "Clog Plant" grows best in bright, indirect light, although quite shaded sites are also survived.

Arranged to the front of bowls of mixed house plants, this plant really comes into its own. The rich dark green leaves contrast well with the lighter greens and variegated leaf colours of the other plants.

When shoots get too long they can be pinched back to encourage more basal branching. These tips from lead shoots provide cutting material.

HYPOCYRTA glabra

KALANCHOE blossfeldiana

Kalanchoe

The *Kalanchoe blossfeldiana* is one of the few plants that has square sections to the flower head. It is very easy to grow and, placed on a light window sill, is almost indestructable. Commercially, great numbers are produced, especially during the winter months, and by regulating the length of daylight these plants can be made to flower at any time of year. Their natural flowering season is February/March although flowers will occur at other times. The popularity of the scarlet forms of *Kalanchoe* in the winter may well be due to their really eye-catching colour under artificial light, which contrasts with the glossy green foliage.

There are a number of new cultivars, with colours from red to pink and from white through cream to yellow. Two recommended kinds growing no more than 18 cm (7 in) high are *K.b.* 'Tetra Vulcan', bright scarlet, and *K.b.* 'Yellow Tom Thumb'. Larger plants and flowers are produced by the Swiss Hybrids. These plants are raised from seed sown in March, the commercial growers covering young plants for part of the day to shorten the day length in July or August to produce flowers from November onwards.

All the composts are suitable, especially the soil based John Innes for ease in home care and good growth. The 9-13 cm (3½-5 in) pot sizes are ample and a minimum winter temperature of 10°C (50°F) is required, although they will survive temperatures as low as 5°C (40°F). Repotting is best done in spring.

Maranta

The moist atmosphere of bottle gardens is perfect for the *Maranta* and its close relative *Calathea*, some species of which are sometimes listed under *Maranta*. Perhaps best known and most widely used as a house plant is *Maranta leuconeura*, growing little more than 15 cm (6 in) high and 30 cm (12 in) in spread. This plant has the unusual habit of folding pairs of leaves together at night like hands in prayer, the reason it has the common name "Prayer Plant". The red veins in the leaves make *M.L. erythrophylla*, more often called *M. tricolor*, even more attractive and both plants must be kept in quite shady to dark conditions to develop their most attractive leaf colourings.

Somewhat larger, reaching 30-50 cm (12-18 in) in height and spread are the several forms of *Calathea*, with one of the most popular, *Calathea mackoyana*, commonly called "Peacock Plant" and occasionally sold as *Maranta mackoyana*, having very attractive leaves. Of the other species, *C. insignis* and *C. louisae* have longer, more slender leaves, light green blotched darker green, and *C. ornata* has leaves with pink veins on the younger leaves, the pink fading to cream with leaf maturity. All the *Calathea* species have purplish undersides to the leaves.

MARANTA leuconeura kerchoveana

MARANTA mackoyana

While a warm, moist atmosphere is best for all these plants they will thrive in the average home atmosphere, especially if efforts are made to provide some moisture for the leaves of *Calathea* every now and then. While they all survive a winter temperature of 10°C (50°F), the higher 13-15°C (55-60°F) will give better growth. Reduce the watering and water content of the compost through the winter and provide a lighter position at this time.

Increase in the speed of growth in summer quickly exhausts the compost and annual repotting and potting on is necessary in the period April to June. Both soil based John Innes No. 2 and the peat based composts are suitable. New plants are obtained by small divisions taken in June and rooted under very warm, moist conditions.

MARANTA leuconeura erythrophylla

Attractive specimens of *M. leuconeura* can be grown in low pans of 16-20 cm (6-8 in) diameter and this plant with its red veined variety is excellent to the front of mixed bowls and in groups of house plants. There can be no better subject for a glass carboy garden. The taller *Calathea* species are attractive specimens in their own right and welcome the damper atmosphere in house plant groups.

Miltonia

MILTONIA 'Salammbo'

You may be surprised to see the *Miltonia* orchid pictures in this, a book of plants for the home and office. I make no apology for this because there are several forms of orchid which require no more moisture in the atmosphere than *Azalea*, *Calathea* and ferns. The "Lady's Slipper" orchid *Cypripedium* is probably the hardiest and both *Cymbidium* and *Miltonia* will thrive in winter temperatures of 13°C (55°F).

These plants require a light position through the winter and some shade from direct sun in mid-summer. The compost must be light, very well aerated and acid. It may be difficult to obtain the special compost made up of 2 parts osmunda fibre and 1 part sphagnum moss required for repotting. The *Cymbidium* and *Cypripedium*, now correctly called *Paphiopedilum!*, require some loam in the compost and you may get away with a mix of 1 part soil and 2 parts very coarse sphagnum peat. It will not be necessary to repot for a couple of years, however, and the exotic orchid flowers are well worth the more competitive price pot grown specimens are offered at today — if only for a couple of years. The Lady's Slipper orchid is another good candidate for the large bottle garden and terrarium.

All that can be done here is to whet your appetite for these exciting flowers, once bitten the search for more detailed information will naturally follow. Like many things in life, orchids are not so difficult to grow once you have had a try.

MILTONIA 'Miami'

Monstera

Large holes and gashes in the rich, shiny green leaves are the interesting attraction of *Monstera deliciosa* which has a string of common names, the most popular being "Mexican Breadfruit Plant" and "Swiss Cheese Plant."

While specimens in 13-15 cm (5-6 in) pots are purchased in great numbers for home decoration, it is the larger specimens grown in larger pots which have the most attractively cut and perforated leaves. The *Monstera* is an easy plant to grow in all standard house plant composts and it requires a minimum winter temperature of 10°C (50°F). However, it survives lower temperatures but new growth comes only when the temperature goes above 18°C (65°F).

The aerial roots that are produced can be left dangling but if directed into the compost and moss wrapped supporting stakes they help improve growth. Given a warm temperature, plenty of moisture and an occasional liquid feed, growth is rapid. This plant deserves space to develop and to be seen at its best.

Water well in summer but allow the compost to dry between watering for the best growth. Repotting is best done in April and a cane or stake will be needed to support stems more than 30 cm (12 in) high.

MONSTERA deliciosa

Neoregelia

NEOREGELIA carolinae 'Tricolor'

NEOREGELIA carolinae 'Marechattii'

The most eye-catching "Bromeliad" leaves are produced by *Neorelegia carolinae* 'Tricolor' and the coloured illustration fully captures the contrast between the red centre and green and cream variegated older leaves. This leaf colour changes again at flowering time when the whole plant turns pink and remains that colour for some time. The green-leaved *N. carolinae* is also known erroneously as *Nidularium meyendorfii.*

Not quite so dramatic but very attractive are the dark green and red-leaved *N. carolinae* 'Marechattii' and the tough dark green-leaved *N. spectabilis,* which has a red spot on the end of each leaf, prompting the common name "Fingernail Plant".

Despite the tropical forest conditions from which they originate, these plants are easy house plants, drawing the moisture they need from the pool of water which must be maintained in the centre of each plant. They require a light, open compost and the proprietary all-peat composts of coarse granulation mixed in equal parts with John Innes No. 2 gives good results. Repotting is best done in late spring.

A light position is needed to give the brightest leaf colour but *Neoregelia* must be kept out of direct sun in mid-summer. Watering must be reduced in winter, when a minimum temperature of 13°C (55°F) is required. A steady temperature of 15°C (60°F) + throughout the year is best, with compost kept just moist.

New plants are produced by potting up the well rooted offsets taken from mature plants at the time of repotting. These offsets will require careful watering and a warm, damp atmosphere until well established. If the compost is too wet rotting occurs.

All the "Bromeliads" look attractive in association with the cork bark sold by florists. Arrange these plants on old tree stumps, boughs of trees and bark by binding sphagnum moss wrapped roots onto the bark with copper wire.

Nephrolepis

NEPHROLEPIS exaltata 'Rooseveltii Plumosa'

All the ferns are increasing in popularity and perhaps the most popular of all greenhouse ferns, the various forms of *Nephrolepis,* deserve wider use in the home today. The soft green foliage, the feel of leaf-covered forest floors and the natural atmosphere provided by the ferns are in perfect contrast to the strong colours of paint and plastic used in modern indoor decor.

There are two forms of *Nephrolepis cordifolia,* the "Sword Fern", worthy of house room, the true species illustrated, and *N.c.* 'Plumosa', which has the ends of the leaflets cut to give a fringed effect. There are a number of *N. exaltata* cultivars with shiny, rich green leaflets, *N.e.* 'Bostoniensis', the "Boston Fern", grows more vigorously than the species, *N.e.* 'Rooseveltii Plumosa' has heavily crested or fringed leaflets, producing the common name "Fluffy Ruffles Fern", and *N.e.* 'Teddy Junior' produces an abundance of leaves which form a thick compact plant.

All the *Nephrolepis* grow well in the all-peat proprietary composts. They are best out of direct sunshine and although a light position is preferable, these and other ferns will survive quite dark situations, even those partly lit artificially.

Plants in a very dry atmosphere will need syringing with water and at no time should the compost be allowed to dry out. Less water will be required in winter when a minimum temperature of 10°C (50°F) is required.

New young plants are produced on stolons from the mature specimen and these can be taken off and potted up in early spring, the time for moving root bound plants into larger pots. In the past these were grown in cane baskets, both free standing and hanging. The graceful foliage no doubt accounts in part for renewed interest in *Nephrolepis* and they still make excellent subjects for hanging baskets, and the larger pot grown plants for specimen use.

NEPHROLEPIS cordifolia

Nertera

NERTERA granadensis

Almost hardy and most aptly named, the "Bead Plant", *Nertera granadensis,* makes an attractive subject in 9 cm (3½ in) pots and in even wider diameter pans. This plant can be used for summer carpet bedding outside, plunging the pot grown specimens, which are covered with the glistening orange berries. If it is grown permanently outside in a sink garden or similar position, some kind of cloche protection will be needed through the winter.

Indoors, *Nertera* grows well in all the potting composts and thrives in most situations, although it is better out of direct sun in mid-summer. Restrict water in the winter and keep a minimum winter temperature of 5°C (40°F). Water freely in summer and give the occasional liquid feed. New plants are raised from seed and by division in early spring.

The leaf form is very similar to that very invasive near weed of the old brick greenhouse *Helxine soleirolii,* with which it should not be confused. The *Helxine,* known appropriately as "Baby's Tears" and "Mind Your Own Business", has both a green and yellow-leaved form and the pink stems root as they grow outwards, completely covering the ground.

Pandanus

PANDANUS veitchii

The "Screw Pines" look something like a cross between a palm and a pineapple but in fact the *Pandanus veitchii* makes a most attractive house plant, growing no more than 65 cm (2 ft) high. For the explanation of the common name we must look to the recurving leaves produced spirally up the stem. This spinal formation eventually leaves a trunk with cork-screw appearance. Two species are used for indoor decoration, *P. sanderi,* rosettes of leaves, green with narrow yellow lines, and *P. veitchii,* slowly producing a trunk and leaves with white line variegation.

Both can be grown in the proprietary peat composts and the soil based composts of John Innes No. 2 strength. A minimum winter temperature of 12°C (55°F) is required and growth commences at the higher summer temperatures, over 18°C (65°F). Keep the compost just damp through the winter and then water more freely with new growth. A light position is needed and potting into larger pots is best done in March/April, eventually reaching a 25 cm (10 in) pot.

New plants are produced from side shoots but high temperatures and propagating frame are needed for this. Both the species make attractive specimens and, whilst a warm, moist atmosphere is best, be careful to avoid water resting at the point where leaf joins stem in cool winter temperatures as this can cause rotting.

PELARGONIUM x domesticum, the "Regal Pelargonium"
(above and right)

PELARGONIUM peltatum, the "Ivy-leaved Geranium", and Pelargonium zonale, the "Zonal Pelargonium"

Pelargonium

Pelargonium x domesticum is better known by the commonly used name "Regal Pelargonium". This makes a beautiful flowering pot plant with many excellent varieties like the rose-red 'Grand Slam', 'Lavender Grand Slam' and the large rose-pink 'Carisbrooke'. These plants provide a mass of flower in May/June and to a lesser extent through to September.

The introduction of new double flowered cultivars has brought the *Pelargonium x hortorum,* also called *P. zonale* and "Zonal Pelargonium", even more into the role of an indoor flowering plant.

Trailing and spreading habit makes the *P. peltatum,* the "Ivy-leaved Geranium", a must for window boxes and hanging baskets but this also makes an attractive flowering pot plant for the window sill, even if a cane is needed for support.

Finally we have the variety of species several of which have scented leaves, for example: *P. crispum* 'Variegatum', the "Lemon-scented Geranium" with leaves edged creamy white, and *P. tomentosum,* the "Peppermint-scented Geranium".

All require a light position, even full sun, and they grow well in both soil based and peat composts. Although the latter may hardly be heavy enough to keep the stronger growing plants upright unless they contain sand. Keep the compost just damp through the winter and maintain a steady low temperature of 8-10°C (45-50°F). Repot in early spring as the period of daylight lengthens and then increase watering and give liquid feed every ten days.

PELLAEA rotundifolia

PELLAEA viridis

PELLIONIA daveauana

Pellaea

Another very attractive fern is the *Pellaea*, with the compact *Pellaea rotundifolia* my favourite, having dark green circular leaflets. An excellent plant for the larger bottle garden. More typically fern-like and twice the size is *P. viridis,* growing to 65 cm (2 ft) in height.

These plants grow well in the all-peat composts and like a warm, moist atmosphere. A minimum winter temperature of 17°C (45°F) is required and it will be easier to keep them looking attractive at a temperature slightly higher than this. Diffuse light and quite shaded sites are acceptable. The compost should be kept damp at all times, increasing the water during the summer. New plants are produced from spores and by division, the former method is certainly best left to the specialist and probably the latter too, unless you are prepared to gamble with an unwanted older plant.

Pellionia

I always thought *Pellionia daveauana* a dull, unimaginative plant when seen hanging in pots from the old stove greenhouses. Careful use can, however, change this plant out of all recognition as the use in the mixed bowl on Back Cover clearly shows. The trailing habit and dark veining of the leaves can be seen there to advantage.

They grow well in the all-peat composts and require a minimum winter temperature of 13°C (55°F). Reduce the watering in winter and increase in summer when temperatures of 18-20°C (65-70°F) give strong growth. New plants are obtained by taking cuttings from the tips of shoots in spring, but very warm, damp conditions are needed for successful rooting.

PEPEROMIA argyreia, syn. PEPEROMIA sandersii   PEPEROMIA caperata   PEPEROMIA magnoliaefolia 'Variegata'

Peperomia

There are very many species of *Peperomia*, a large number being suited to indoor cultivation in pots. They have long slender flower spikes, rather like upright mouse-tails, and in one or two species the flowers are quite a feature, for example *P. caperata*, with the white flower spikes contrasting against dark green, velvet-textured leaves.

Many of them originate from tropical South America and they are at home in warm, moist conditions. The comparatively small, undemanding root system is easily damaged by overwatering and care should be taken not to do this to excess. Once acclimatised to room conditions they do make excellent house plants.

The three species illustrated at the top of this page represent the best qualities in the genera and another, *Peperomia scandens* has bright cream variegated leaves, its trailing and, if supported, climbing habit eventually reaching 1 m (3 ft).

They grow well in John Innes No. 1 Potting Compost and the proprietary composts, seldom needing a pot larger than 9 cm (3½ in). They should be kept on the dry side through the winter and although they survive a minimum winter temperature of 10°C (50°F) they are easier to care for at 13°C (55°F).

Provide a light position out of direct sunlight in summer and the occasional repotting of mature plants is best done in late spring. New plants are produced from cuttings, those species producing stems, like *P. scandens*, from stem cuttings and the remainder from that fascinating method of rooting the leaves and leaf stalks.

Philodendron

The genera *Philodendron* is a most valuable addition to the range of plants for indoor decoration. It has a variety of habits and leaf forms that are best described in three groups. First and perhaps best known is *Philodendron scandens,* a climbing or trailing plant with aerial roots, light green leaves and the common name "Sweetheart Plant". This name no doubt comes from the heart-shaped leaves and perhaps its very easy nature. In fact all *Philodendron* species are so adaptable to home and office conditions they can all be described as easy to grow and attractive in appearance.

Similar in habit, with climbing form and aerial roots are a range of larger leaved species, several of which have been intercrossed to produce hybrids and attractive cultivars. The rich red/bronze young leaves of *P.e.* 'Burgundy' and dark green of *P. x mandaianum* are excellent examples. A recent introduction *P.* 'Tuxla' has large spear shaped leaves on thick fleshy stems, its bushy growth is attractive and easy to look after.

Some of these cultivars have been given the well suited common name of "Elephant's Ear" although for me they are more like arum lily leaves, a not surprising fact when we realise that all come from the arum family. Others have deeply notched leaves like *P. panduriforme.*

Quite different in form is the third group with bushy, not climbing, habit and deeply cut, large leaves. Good examples are *P. selloum, P. pinnatifidum* and the most widely grown *P. bipinnatifidum,* which is a very tough and resilient indoor plant. If you look carefully at the illustration of *P. selloum* it will be seen the young leaves are complete and of typical arum heart shape. It is the mature leaves which are some 50 cm (18 in) across and deeply cut.

The all-peat composts and soil based types with added peat are suitable for all *Philodendron.* While *P. scandens* is a useful house plant as a young specimen in 9 cm (3½ in) pots it will, given support, eventually grow to form a 1-2 m (3-6 ft) specimen requiring a pot of 15 cm (6 in) diameter. All the larger leaved forms will need pots from 15-25 cm (6-10 in) diameter to develop and show their true form. A piece of cork bark or moss-filled cylinder of plastic netting is needed to provide a natural support for the climbing forms and to provide a resting place for some of the aerial roots.

PHILODENDRON x mandaianum

PHILODENDRON panduriforme

Keep out of direct sunlight, apart from this plants grow well in both light and quite dark positions. Watering should be restricted in winter to keep the compost just damp, increasing in the summer when growth is more rapid. A minimum winter temperature of 13°C (55°F) is recommended, lower temperatures will be survived for short periods. A warmer temperature than 13°C will make cultivation easier.

Sponge the leaves occasionally with a damp cloth to provide some humidity around the plant and to keep the leaves clean, shiny and attractive. Repot about every second year in spring, do not be in too much of a hurry to repot, quite large specimens can be grown in the 15 cm (6 in) pots. The larger leaved forms do extremely well in the self-watering containers and are ideal for offices, hotels and other rooms in public buildings.

Little pruning and cutting back is necessary, except perhaps pinching out the tips of young plants of *P. scandens* to encourage plenty of basal shoots. The longer trailing shoots of this species should also be tied in to keep the plant compact and shapely. All the climbing forms can be propagated by cuttings and layers and the bushy forms are seed raised. Except perhaps for *P. scandens* this raising of new plants is best left to the specialist.

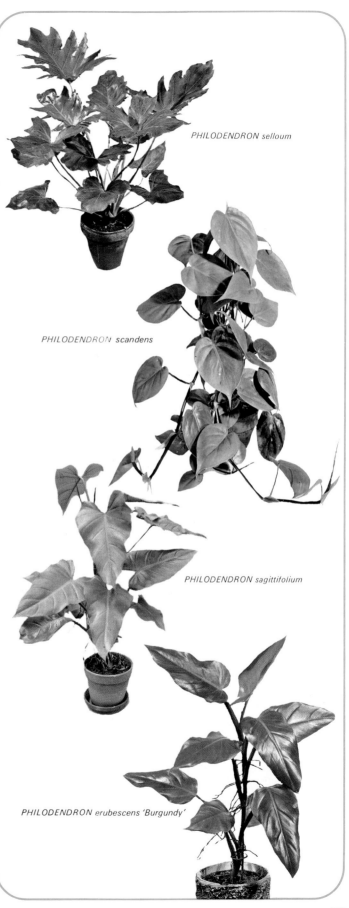

PHILODENDRON *selloum*

PHILODENDRON *scandens*

PHILODENDRON *sagittifolium*

PHILODENDRON *erubescens 'Burgundy'*

PHŒNIX canariensis

Phoenix

This palm from the Canary Islands, *Phoenix canariensis*, is useful if you wish to create a sub-tropical date palm effect. Mature specimens reach 5 m (15 ft) in height and 3 m (9 ft) spread and smaller pot grown plants need plenty of room. Both the *P. canariensis* and the true "Date Palm", *P. dactylifera* which some people like to raise from stones, grow well in the soil based John Innes Compost No. 2. While the date palm requires a minimum winter temperature of 10°C (50°F) *P. canariensis* will thrive at a temperature several degrees lower although its 'feet' must always be kept warm.

Watering should be restricted during the semi dormant winter period, watering more often in spring and autumn and watering freely in summer, when a fortnightly liquid feed can be given. Repotting is best done in April and either very large pots or tubs will be needed for the well established specimens.

These palms are raised from seed but a warm, 20°C (70°F), moist atmosphere is needed for several months. February and March are the best months to sow seed. If you require a somewhat smaller palm *P. robelinii* with its very fine graceful leaves should be chosen. This plant of bushy rather than tree-like habit is more suited to the smaller indoor situation, eventually reaching 1-2 m (3-6 ft).

Pilea

Commonly called "Aluminium Plant", the *Pilea cadierei* has a metallic marking to the leaves. It is very easy to grow but is most attractive either as a young plant or a larger plant well pinched so that it has plenty of young growth. Less attractive but equally easy to grow is *Pilea muscosa*, with much divided frondy leaves and yellowish-green flowers throughout the summer. Puffs of pollen are expelled from the flower anthers of *P. muscosa*, no doubt explaining the common names "Artillery Plant" and "Gunpowder Plant". Slightly more demanding in cultural treatment is *Pilea mollis*, the "Moon Valley Plant" with more velvety leaves and a *Coleus*-like appearance.

All potting composts are suitable and a winter temperature of 10°C (50°F) is required. Do not let the compost dry out and keep these plants away from direct sunlight in mid-summer. The *Pilea* will stand quite shaded conditions in the home. A good subject to use in mixed bowls and in troughs with other pot grown foliage plants.

Platycerium

One of the most dramatic of all ferns and a very eye-catching house plant is *Platycerium alcicorne*, also listed as *P. bifurcatum* and very aptly called "Stag's-horn Fern". The name is so apt because plants can be knocked out of their pots, the soil ball wrapped in sphagnum moss and then bound to a board or piece of cork bark with copper wire. This produces a plant growing out from the board just like mounted stag's horns and it can be hung from walls and similar superstructures.

Such moss-wrapped plants must be taken down regularly, soaked in water and allowed to drain before returning to the decorative position. A sheet of thin polythene can be wrapped round the block of wood and held in place with hairpins after soaking to prevent wet marks on the wall.

Pot grown plants grow well in the all-peat composts and they require a minimum winter temperature of 10°C (50°F). Excellent subjects to fill hanging baskets, but they require the occasional syringing with water and sponging with a damp cloth to provide a moist atmosphere around the leaves.

PLATYCERIUM alcicorne

Primula

Take my advice and use some of the very attractive *Primula* species if you want easy plants to grow and beautiful pastel shaded flowers in winter and spring. Easiest of all and tremendously improved over the past few years is the "Primrose", *Primula acaulis*. Breeding programmes have brought increased flower size and extensive range of colour from the various primroses and polyanthus in cultivation, such that the modern mixtures like *P.a.* 'Europa', *P.a.* 'Biedermeier' and *P.a.* 'Aalsmeer' are quite startling in their beauty and fresh primrose fragrance. Not only can you enjoy these primroses in flower indoors in winter and early spring, but once they have flowered the plants can be gradually acclimatised to colder outdoor temperatures before planting in the garden to flower again outside the following spring.

PRIMULA sinensis

PRIMULA acaulis

There are four other *Primula* species that have been used for many years to provide colour indoors in winter and spring. The least well known and tallest of the four is *Primula x kewensis*, with circles of clear yellow, fragrant flowers carried above light green leaves which are covered with a white powdery material, called farina. More recent introductions are virtually free of this farina.

Beautiful and delicate in appearance but quite hardy in the home are the freely produced flower spikes of *Primula malacoides*, commonly called the "Fairy Primula". Even tougher and with much larger flowers is the *Primula obconica*. Once again extensive breeding work has increased the quantity of flower produced and the range of colour and we now have orange, purple and blue shades as well as the well known red, pink and white cultivars.

Last but by no means least, there is *Primula sinensis*, a neat compact plant with shorter flower stems and very attractive leaves. The older cultivars of this plant need careful handling because of their tendency to insecure rooting. More recent introduction like *P.s.* 'Empress Mixed' are much improved and the foliage is non irritant to sensitive skins.

People who have sensitive skin are well advised to avoid growing all but *Primula acaulis* and *P.s.* 'Empress Mixed'. The *Primula obconica* is such a good indoor plant it is a great shame it causes a stinging nettle-like rash on a few people but if this plant causes you discomfort enjoy *Primula acaulis* types without harm.

All these *Primula* species grow well in John Innes Potting Compost No. 1 and the proprietary peat based potting composts. They require cool conditions for the best results and temperatures 8-10°C (45-50°F) are ideal. Keep nicely damp at all times and feeding is not required. *P. obconica* wilts when allowed to dry out and quickly recovers when watered again. If you have trouble watering plants, *P. obconica* is for you, just water at the first sign of wilting. These plants in soil based compost flower for months in all kinds of indoor situations.

The "Primroses" are especially attractive to the front of mixed bowls of house plants and indoor dish gardens. After they have flowered the primroses can be replaced by *Saintpaulia* for summer and autumn flowers.

Propagation of all five kinds is by seed sown late spring/early summer. Be sure seed is in a cool position because germination is prevented by high temperatures, that is, above 17°C (65°F). While *P. obconica* can be potted on in April to provide a second year's growth and flowering all plants are best treated as expendable after the first season of indoor flowering.

PRIMULA *malacoides*

PRIMULA *obconica*

Pteris

PTERIS multifida

This genera contains many fern species and cultivars used for indoor decoration. The type is best known by *P. cretica*, the "Ribbon Fern", similar in appearance to *P. multifida*. Both are referred to in the nursery trade as "Majors". Other similar types but with crested edges to the fronds come under the heading *P. cretica* 'Wimsettii'.

Several forms have white to silver linear variegation down the fronds and these are most attractive. Examples include *Pteris ensiformis* 'Victoriae', the broader, cut-edge fronds of *P. quadriaurita argyraea* and *P. cretica albo-lineata*. Easiest of all to grow, with large fronds somewhat bracken-like in appearance is *Pteris tremula*. This fern produces masses of brown spores on the underside of the fronds in the autumn when the leaves take on a dull appearance. New growth soon replaces this, however, and the plant becomes bright green again.

The *Pteris* grows well in the all-peat composts and requires a winter temperature of 12°C (55°F), *P. cretica* and *P. tremula* withstanding temperatures down to 7°C (45°F). Keep the compost damp at all times, giving less water in the winter. New plants are raised from spores, a job best left to the skilled fern propagator. Given a position out of direct sun in high summer these ferns are very easy and useful indoor house plants.

PTERIS ensiformis 'Victoriae'

PTERIS cretica albo-lineata

Rhoeo

Another plant happy in shaded parts of the room is *Rhoeo discolor* and the more attractive *R.d.* 'Vittatum', which has creamy yellow lines on the leaves. The insignificant white flowers are produced in broad boat-shaped bracts in the axils of the leaves at various times of the year on established plants. These bracts are deep purple, the same colour as the undersides of the leaves.

Young specimens are the most attractive, with new plants obtained by rooting basal shoots from mature plants in April. The *Rhoeo* grows well in John Innes Potting Compost. A 13-15 cm (5-6 in) pot will be needed. This size of pot balances the erect leaves which are 30 cm (12 in) long. A winter temperature of 7-10°C (45-50°F) is all that is required by this undemanding plant.

RHOEO *discolor* 'Vittatum'

ROCHEA *coccinea*

Rochea

It is a toss-up whether this plant joins the succulents, but cultural treatments are very similar to several other flowering house plants, so here it rests. Commercial nurseries gently force *Rochea coccinea*, also listed as *Crassula coccinea*, to flower early spring. It will flower late spring/early summer without additional heat.

Stems 24-30 cm (12-18 in) high carry the heads of brilliant flowers, which are long lasting indoors. There are other species with white and yellow flowers. After flowering the plants are cut back to produce new basal shoots which carry the next year's flowers. These young shoots can also be used to provide cuttings which are rooted in late spring/early summer to produce new plants.

The *Rochea* grows well in John Innes Potting Compost No. 2 and requires a winter temperature of 5-7°C (40-45°F). Keep the compost just moist through the winter and step up watering in the summer.

Saintpaulia

The common name "African Violet", the sumptuous flowers with bright yellow stamens, the succulent leaves and the virtually continuous flowering make *Saintpaulia ionantha* cultivars increasingly popular. More recently introduced forms are resistant to flower dropping, flower more profusely and for a longer period.

These plants grow well in the proprietary all-peat composts, with young plants fully accommodated in 9 cm (3½ in) pots and the larger specimens best in the 13-15 cm (5-6 in) pans and half pots. A warm damp atmosphere in a light position out of direct light is the ideal. Whilst the *Saintpaulia* will survive temperatures occasionally lower than the recommended minimum of 13°C (55°F) they are much easier to keep in good condition at 15°C (60°F).

Correct watering is the other important factor once the right temperature and light position is provided. While the plants are flowering see that the compost is kept nicely moist.

This is easy to determine where plants are grown in thin plastic pots and the all-peat composts because dry plants are very light in weight — less than 120 gm (4 oz) — and at this weight they need watering to approximately 170 gm (5½ oz). After a good flush of flowering the plants should be kept on the dry side for 4-6 weeks when a new batch of flower buds will be seen and normal moisture levels can be resumed.

Better to keep a fraction on the dry side than overwater, which causes the leaf stem to rot. Plunging the pots in a bowl of damp peat and keeping the peat damp provides the ideal moist atmosphere for *Saintpaulia*.

Sansevieria

Really striking upright foliage, along with the common name "Mother-in-law's Tongue", and the way this plant thrives in neglect explains the widespread use and popularity of *Sansevieria*. The species *S. trifasciata* has mottled green leaves and the boldly yellow-edged form *S.t.* 'Laurentii' grows taller, to 1 m (3 ft) or more. If a more dwarf and compact form is required with more circular leaves and well balanced rosette of growth the *S.t.* 'Hahnii' should be chosen.

The *Sansevieria* is best in full sun but will thrive in quite shaded situations. It grows well in the soil based John Innes Potting Compost No. 2 and the proprietary peat composts. The soil based ones are best, especially for larger specimens where the weight is needed to balance the quite heavy, tall leaves. Always keep the compost on the dry side, especially in winter. It is quite in order for the roots to really fill the pot and there is no hurry to repot.

If you want the plants to keep producing new leaves hold a temperature of 15°C (60°F). They will thrive in lower winter temperatures, say 10°C (50°F) and survive short spells as low as 7°C (45°F). Really this plant is very easy and the only danger is overwatering. Grow a big pot full of leaves for attractive specimens which are a feature in modern furniture settings. Smaller plants give height to arrangements in bowls.

SANSEVIERIA trifasciata 'Hahnii'

New plants are obtained by dividing off well rooted side shoots. Plants can also be raised from sections of leaf but these will all be green-leaved, even if the leaf sections have the golden variegation.

The Sansevieria has thick fleshy rhizomatous roots which are so powerful that when they produce side shoots they can distort a plastic pot with their pressure and if forced downwards in a clay or plastic pot will lift the plant and the ball of soil right out of the pot. The only action to take then is to sever the powerful side shoot with a sharp knife and replace the plant firmly in its pot.

SANSEVIERIA trifasciata 'Laurentii'

Saxifraga stolonifera 'Tricolor'

Saxifraga

We can certainly label *Saxifraga stolonifera* 'Tricolor', also known as *S. sarmentosa* 'Tricolor', easy and even more indestructable than *Sansevieria.* The name stolonifera refers to the plant's habit of producing quantities of young plants on stolons like strawberry runners. These runners hang from the main plant and are an attractive feature in themselves, no doubt prompting the common name "Mother of Thousands".

The younger specimens are to me the most attractive and new runners need potting up every now and then to ensure a supply of attractive plants. These plants grow well in the soil based composts and all the potting composts are suitable. The *Saxifraga* is almost hardy and will thrive in winter temperatures as low as 7°C (45°F). It produces quite tall flower stems with masses of small white flowers but it is the red and cream variegated leaves of *S.s.* 'Tricolor' that are the feature of this plant.

A perfect candidate for a hanging cane pot plant holder, where the runners can trail from above and make an attractive feature. Keep the plant well watered throughout the year and in a light position out of direct sun in mid-summer. A fortnightly liquid feed through the summer months is also an advantage.

Schefflera

The "Umbrella Tree", *Schefflera actinophylla,* is a relatively recent introduction and is a valuable house plant when placed against a light background to show up the glossy leaflets which radiate from the stem like the ribs of an umbrella. Given time, it will grow to quite a size, some 2 m (6 ft) high.

Both the soil based and proprietary peat composts are suitable and *Schefflera* requires a minimum temperature of 12°C (55°F). The best growth occurs in a well lit position out of direct sunlight in mid-summer. This plant will also survive in quite shaded situations. Keep the compost nicely moist throughout the year, increasing the water in summer and in atmospheres with higher temperatures.

It is advisable to pot on every other year until a 17-19 cm (6-8 in) pot is reached, liquid feeding on alternate weeks through the summer in those years without repotting. New plants are raised from seed, a job best left with the specialist because high temperatures are needed.

SCHEFFLERA actinophylla

Scindapsus

A close relative of the *Philodendron* and of similar appearance, *Scindapsus aureus* has a climbing and trailing habit. The leaves are attractively streaked yellow and there are three other forms in cultivation, *S.a.* 'Golden Queen', with bolder leaf markings, *S.a.* 'Marble Queen' which has cream variegated leaves and *S.a.* 'Silver Queen', with leaves that are almost white.

The *Scindapsus* grows well in the all-peat and soil based composts. They require a light position to get the best variegated leaf colour but must be kept out of strong direct sunlight. A minimum winter temperature of 10°C (50°F) is required, with good leaf appearance more easily maintained at temperatures a degree or two higher.

If the plants become rather straggly and some of the leaf edges brown due to excessive watering and exposure to strong sunlight, cut the plants back by at least half in April and May to encourage new growth from the base. New plants are produced by rooted cuttings taken from the top of strong growing shoots but warm conditions, 20°C (70°F) are needed for this.

These plants are good in mixed bowls, grown as specimens and they grow attractively when supported on cork bark or trained up a mossed stake or other similar natural materials.

SCINDAPSUS aureus

Sedum

While it could be argued that *Sedum sieboldii* should be listed with the succulents, it requires treatment very similar to other foliage plants. The green leaved species is nowhere near as attractive as *Sedum sieboldii* 'Medio-variegatum', which has the addition on the leaves of bold splashes of creamy white. The leaves on both these *Sedum* species are interestingly arranged in whorls of three round the stem and pink flowers are produced in the autumn.

Use a free draining compost and one not too rich in fertiliser, for example John Innes Potting Compost No. 1. Water freely in the summer but reduce through the winter. Repotting is best done in spring, although quite sizeable specimens can be grown in 9 cm (3½ in) pots. These plants grow well in full sun and require a minimum winter temperature of 5°C (45°F). New Plants are produced by rooting cuttings in spring and early summer.

Sedum makes an attractive plant in the smaller pots and pans. House plant containers which allow the trailing habit to develop unheeded and yet present the plant to be seen from above are ideal.

SEDUM sieboldii 'Medio-variegatum'

BELOPERONE guttata, PILEA cadierei and FICUS pumila.

Senecio (Cineraria)

The *Senecio cruentus*, better known to most people as *Cineraria cruenta*, is another most valuable winter flowering plant. Recently introduced hybrids are more compact and have an excellent range of colour. Careful selection of strain allows an extension of flower season from Christmas to May.

A light position, careful watering and steady cool temperature are needed to ensure maximum flower life indoors. Once the plant has flowered it is discarded, new plants being raised each year from seed sown in July and August. If you raise seed at home and want a succession of flowering, choose an early flowering strain like *S.c.* 'Brilliant Mixed' and a later strain like *S.c.* 'Royalty'.

All composts are suitable, including John Innes Potting Compost No. 2 and the proprietary all-peat ones. It is best if room temperatures do not exceed 12°C (55°F) for longest flower life and a minimum winter temperature of 7°C (45°F) is recommended. While these plants will require regular watering through the winter, be careful not to overwater or leave the pots standing in water. Greenfly can be quite a pest on home grown plants and regular spraying is recommended to prevent attack.

SENECIO cruentus

SENECIO macroglossus variegatus

Senecio

Often mistaken for the common ivy, *Senecio macroglossus variegatus* is a very easy, quick growing climber which makes an ideal house plant. It has the common name "Cape Ivy" which is much easier to cope with than the tongue-twisting latinname.

This plant grows well in all the potting composts and requires a minimum winter temperature of 10°C (50°F). It will thrive in all positions and is better out of direct sun in mid-summer. New plants are produced from cuttings which root very easily. Drop a piece of shoot into a glass of water and in time roots will begin to form. Where plants get too straggly and lose lower leaves, cut the plant hard back in spring and early summer and new growth will be made from the base.

Try growing this plant in the hanging containers like jungle jars where the twining stems will climb the supports as well as trail over the sides of the container. It can also be grown to advantage in hanging baskets. Watch out for greenfly attack and spray with any of the house plant pest killers to keep this *Senecio* clean.

Sinningia (Gloxinia)

The thick, succulent leaves and stems and the rich velvety trumpet flowers of *Sinningia speciosa* hybrids are most attractive and make the "Gloxinia" a very popular indoor plant. It requires treatment very similar to the tuberous *Begonia* and corms of both are usually offered for sale together in spring. In addition to the flower colours illustrated there are hybrids with bicolour flowers, one colour in the form of many spots over the outer rim of the trumpet. Some double flowered hybrids have become available in recent years.

Warm temperatures, 20-22°C (70-75°F), are needed early in the year to start the tubers into growth. Once well established the temperatures can be dropped to 18°C (64°F), the recommended average for good growth throughout the summer. These plants thrive in the proprietary all-peat composts and grow well in the 13-15 cm (5-6 in) half pots and pans, the wider base of these pans providing overall stability in the lightweight compost.

Keep "Gloxinias" in a light position out of strong direct sunshine in summer. Once growth is vigorous water regularly and keep the compost nicely moist throughout the growing season. After flowering reduce the watering and allow the tubers to dry off before removing from the compost and storing in a frost-free place to start into growth the following spring.

An indication of the colour range in modern "Gloxinia" cultivars

Solanum

Christmas is the time for *Solanum capsicastrum*, commonly called "Winter Cherry", when the berries are a shiny bright scarlet. While they are used for indoor decoration from December to January place in a light position with a minimum temperature of 7-10°C (45-50°F). In spring when the berries have lost their brightness the plants can be cut back by one half, potted on into a size larger pot and stood outside to make new growth, flower and set berries for another winter's use.

The plants need spraying with water when in flower to help the flowers to set. Spraying the plants with the proprietary tomato set chemical will also help the formation of fruits. Once berries have set ensure they are kept well watered and give a liquid feed every 10-14 days. Lack of food and dryness cause premature leaf fall. Bring plants indoors before the chance of frost and see the compost is kept just nicely damp through the winter.

New plants are raised from seed sown in early spring. Such seedlings are potted into 10 cm (4 in) pots filled with John Innes Potting Compost No. 2 and the tips pinched out at least once when the plants are 7 cm (3 in) high to encourage well branched growth.

SOLANUM capsicastrum

SPARMANNIA africana

Sparmannia

Planted in the greenhouse border soil *Sparmannia africana* will reach over 2 m (6 ft) in height and spread. A member of the "Lime" family and commonly called either "House Lime" or "African Hemp", it is more restrained when pot grown, with specimens reaching 0.6-1 m (2-3 ft) in height in 15 cm (6 in) diameter pots. Clusters of single white flowers with prominent stamens are produced in early summer.

Use a fairly rich compost such as the soil based John Innes No. 3 Potting Compost and if retaining plants into a second year for indoor decoration repot in April or May. They require plenty of moisture through the summer to support the growth of lush foliage, the leaves being some 20 cm (8 in) across. Reduce the water in winter but keep the compost just nicely damp. Provide a light sunny position, but shaded from direct sun, in mid-summer.

Plants can be cut hard back in spring to produce new growth from the base. The tips of such new growth provide cutting material which can be rooted to produce new plants.

Spathiphyllum

The rich, dark green leaves of *Spathiphyllum wallisii* are quite as attractive to me as leaves of plants like *Aspidistra* and *Cissus*. We have the added, benefit, from May to August, of bright white arum-like bracts with *Spathiphyllum*, the bracts which are long lasting, surrounding the centrally arranged flowers on the stem. The larger flowered and larger leaved *S.x.* 'Mauna Loa' grows 0.5-0.6 m (2-3 ft).

Both the soil based and the all-peat composts are suitable for this plant, and a 13 cm (5 in) diameter pot is ample for all but the largest specimen. Any repotting is best done in spring and the *Spathiphyllum* responds to the moisture provided by plunging the pot in a bowl of damp peat. Keep the compost damp all the year round and give more water in summer. A light position is needed through the winter and a more shaded site in summer. Certainly keep out of direct sun in mid-summer.

Provide a minimum winter temperature of 10°c (50°F) although a few degrees lower will be survived for short periods. Wipe the leaves with a damp cloth occasionally to retain the glossy appearance and to provide additional humidity.

SPATHIPHYLLUM wallisii

STEPHANOTIS floribunda

Stephanotis

One of the most sweetly scented indoor flowering plants, *Stephanotis floribunda* also has attractive evergreen leaves. Beautiful specimens are sold in shops and garden centres with the climbing stem wound round wire and bamboo cane supports wreathed in flowers. It will be necessary to maintain a warm temperature and give the right cultural treatment to maintain the attractive appearance and encourage the production of more flowers.

A minimum winter temperature of (50°F) is needed and a few more degrees of warmth are a help. Much warmer temperatures are needed through the summer when a minimum of 18°C (65°F) should be provided. While both the soil based John Innes Compost No. 2 and the proprietary peat based composts are suitable, plants seem to flower better in the home where composts with a low lime or chalk content are used. Certainly lime-free water, either rainwater or distilled water, should be used. In summer water freely and syringe the plants occasionally in an attempt to provide a warm, damp atmosphere. Keep just moist through the winter especially at the lower temperatures.

Where side growths are getting too large they can be cut back to within 8 cm (3 in) of the main stem in early spring.

Streptocarpus

Leaf propagation, making cuttings from portions of leaf and producing new plants from these, is the method used to increase *Streptocarpus*. These plants require treatment similar to "Gloxinia" and until recently were very much subjects for the heated greenhouse.

Breeding work at the John Innes Research Institute is rapidly changing this situation and their hybrids with girls' names, for example 'Diana', cerise; 'Fiona', pink; and 'Louise', deep blue-violet; are excellent indoor flowering plants. Given the warmth of central heating, the John Innes hybrids are very free flowering from April to October.

The leaves are long and strap-shaped, a little too long on some of the first hybrids. All *Streptocarpus* grow well in the proprietary peat composts and they need a minimum winter temperature of 10°C (55°F). Keep the plants just moist through the winter and increase watering in summer. The plants are best repotted and potted on to larger pots in Spring although younger plants in pots up to the 13 cm (5 in) size are the most attractive.

Plants of *Streptocarpus* can be raised from seed but, like *Begonia* and *Sinningia*, the seed is very small and requires high temperatures and the correct cultural conditions in early spring for success.

A range of the colours available in Streptocarpus x hybridus

SYAGRUS weddeliana

Syagrus (Cocos)

The dwarf palm *Syagrus weddeliana*, widely listed as *Cocos weddeliana*, is often used for indoor decoration. Young plants in pots are attractive because of the finely cut leaves and with root restriction they grow little more than 30 cm (12 in) high. Specimens with unrestricted growth will reach 2 m (6 ft) in height.

A warm temperature is needed for *Syagrus*, 15°C (60°F) in winter and ideally a damp atmosphere. Soil based potting compost and the proprietary peat composts are suitable and should be used when repotting, every second or third year, in spring. Block up the drainage hole to prevent the tap root growing through and being damaged. A fairly light position is needed out of direct sun in mid-summer and whilst they require regular watering in summer, cut back in autumn and spring and keep just damp in winter. New plants are raised from seed at very high temperatures.

Small seedlings are useful plants for the bottle garden and terrarium where the humidity and warmth suits them.

Syngonium

Typical, heart-shaped arum leaves are the feature of *Syngonium podophyllum* and no doubt prompt the common name "Goose Foot Plant". Left without support they produce short jointed plants but given cork bark or a column of sphagnum moss wrapped in plastic netting in which the aerial roots can grow, attractive climbing specimens very similar to *Philodendron* can be produced. In addition to the dark green leaved species there are forms with light and dark green variegated leaves, for example *S.p.* 'Emerald Gem'.

All potting composts are suitable and the proprietary all-peat ones ideal. A minimum winter temperature of 12°C (59°F) is required and these plants are happier in warmer temperatures. Water freely in the summer and occasionally syringe the leaves or sponge with water, reduce the watering in winter and keep just damp. Place in a light position for the best results but out of direct sun in mid-summer.

Syngonium is attractive when arranged with other decorative foliage plants, in an arrangement they welcome the additional humidity of the atmosphere.

SYNGONIUM podophyllum 'Emerald Gem'

Thunbergia

You can have no better plant for a sunny summer window than the annual climber *Thunbergia alata*, known by the common name of "Black-eyed Susan". Masses of the attractive single flowers with black centres are produced from June to September. Young plants in 9 cm (3½ in) pots grow rapidly in spring and canes are needed to support the twining shoots.

All the potting composts are suitable and a summer temperature of 15°C (60°F) and above is required. Water freely once the young plants are well established and liquid feed every 10 to 14 days through the summer. All plants are seed raised, sowing early spring in a temperature of 18°C (65°F). Like other annual flowering plants the "Black-eyed Susan" is discarded at the end of the summer.

These plants may have a short life but they really give colour for money. In addition to pot grown plants on the window sill they can be grown in hanging baskets, where they climb the support chains, in window boxes, tubs and in sheltered garden borders in the warmer climatic areas.

THUNBERGIA alata

Tradescantia

TRADESCANTIA fluminensis 'Variegata'

Probably the easiest and most widely grown indoor plants are the various forms of *Tradescantia fluminensis*. While the green-leaved species is the easiest of all, the variegated leaf forms like *T.f.* 'Variegata', green striped white and flushed pink, are more attractive. It is necessary to pinch out any all-green shoots on these variegated plants to prevent the stronger growing green shoots taking over completely. Larger leaved and with thicker stems, the cultivar 'Rochford's Quicksilver' has the advantage of never reverting to green.

All potting composts are suitable and the *Tradescantia* is best in a light position out of strong sunlight mid-summer. Whilst very easy to grow, care should be taken to see that these plants do not dry out and are not scorched by hot sun because this causes unsightly brown leaf tips. While they survive cool winter conditions down to 7°C (45°F) they grow faster and are easier to care for at higher temperatures.

Young stock, growing vigorously, that is the way to keep these plants attractive. Young growing tips snapped off mature plants root very quickly, even in a glass of water on the window sill. Once rooted the "Wandering Jew" as this plant is commonly called can be planted in pots and bowls to trail over the edge of the container. It is a very attractive subject for hanging baskets and a good plant for children to grow.

TRADESCANTIA 'Rochford's Quicksilver'

Vriesia

The last "Bromeliad" in our selection has really brilliant and long lasting scarlet bracts to the flower spike. The leaves of *Vriesia splendens* are also attractive in their own right, with light and dark green zebra stripes. There are several other species which make attractive house plants, including *V. hieroglyphica,* the "King of the Bromeliads", which has light green leaves barred purple, green bracts and yellow flowers on a flowering stem 75 cm (2½ ft) high; and *V.* 'Rodigasiana', yellow flowers and bracts yellow flushed red on spikes 30 cm (1 ft) high.

All-peat composts are ideal for these plants, which are best grown in warm damp atmospheres. A minimum winter temperature of 12°C (55°F) is required and growth will be better if slightly higher temperatures are maintained. Plants will survive lower temperatures, even down to 7°C (45°F) but the moisture in the compost will need to be reduced under such conditions.

Flowered plants will produce new flowering shoots if grown on for another season or two. Propagation is from seed, the seedlings taking many years to flower and from side shoots, but propagation is not easy and best left to the specialist.

Coming from tropical forest conditions the *Vriesia* will tolerate heavily shaded positions and should not be exposed to direct strong sunshine.

VRIESIA splendens

VALLOTA *purpurea*

Vallota

One of the few evergreen bulbs which can be grown on the sunny window sill is *Vallota speciosa*, also listed as *Vallota purpurea* and commonly called "Scarborough Lily". The large, thick strap-shaped leaves are quite striking in their own right but the glorious luminant orange-scarlet flowers in July and August are superb.

The *Vallota* is best grown in soil based compost of John Innes No. 1 fertiliser content. Do not repot or pot on until the pot is absolutely full of roots. Such repotting is best done after flowering in September/October. Keep just damp through the late autumn and early winter, increasing the watering in late winter and spring. Reduce somewhat in the summer before flowering. A warm, sunny window sill is the spot for this bulb. New plants are obtained by detaching small side bulbs when repotting. Such side shoots should be potted into 9 cm (3½ in) pots of John Innes Compost No. 1 and treated in the same way as larger specimens. If by chance the strap-shaped leaves do not appeal then cut the beautiful flower spikes and arrange in water, as has been done in this illustration. The old flower stem should be cut from plants when yellow and withering.

ZEBRINA *pendula*

Zebrina

Closely related to *Tradescantia* and often confused with it is *Zebrina pendula* with mid-green and silver upper surface to the leaves and rich purple beneath. For even brighter colour choose *Z.p.* 'Quadricolor', which has a rose purple line in addition on the upper leaf surface. Young, strongly growing plants are by far the most attractive and long straggling stems, bare at the base, should be pinched back. The tips from such pinching back are easily rooted to produce more plants.

All potting composts are suitable and the compost should be kept just nicely damp through the winter, increasing the watering in summer when a fortnightly liquid feed is recommended. Repot in April, the best time to root cuttings for new stock, and keep the plants away from hot direct sun in summer.

A minimum winter temperature of 13°C (55°F) is recommended but warmer temperatures and a light position in winter will give better growth. This is especially important for the more demanding *Z.p.* 'Quadricolor'. Just the plant for the front of mixed bowls, to grow in pots to trail over the edge of house plant troughs and for hanging containers. It is also excellent, if kept regularly pinched, in hanging baskets.

CACTI AND SUCCULENTS

Most succulents make excellent plants for the home since they are designed to tolerate all kinds of adverse conditions, such as dry air and lack of water. Generally speaking cacti need less heat than other succulents during the winter months and accordingly less water. Within the overall category of Succulents it is usual to distinguish cacti from other succulents. The distinction is based on a botanical feature common to all Cacti but not found on succulents called an Areole. The areole is the small tuft of felt or hair at the base of the spine and even though many succulents other than cacti have some sort of spine only the true cacti have this curious felted base.

During the summer cacti need to be treated just like any other type of pot plant and if grown on a sunny windowsill with plenty of fresh air and warmth may need watering as often as twice a week. When watering you must take particular care to ensure that the pot ball is thoroughly soaked; failure to do this can result in the build up of sour patches in which fungal diseases can grow and kill the plant. It is best to soak each pot thoroughly in a bowl of water, holding the surface of the soil below the water level until the bubbles stop rising. Succulents other than cacti will respond well to similar treatment although some of the pebbles type succulents, such as *Conophytums,* may have to be rested during the summer.

During the winter most cacti will need to be rested. The exceptions are of course Christmas Cacti. They should be taken away from their summer position and ideally placed on a north facing windowsill in a relatively cool room, for example a spare bedroom. The temperature should ideally fall to around 40°F (5°C) and the plants should be kept absolutely dry. If it is not practicable to keep as low a temperature as this some shrivelling of the plant may occur and in this case water should be given immediately. But remember cacti must be compelled to rest if they are to flower prolifically the following summer. Succulents other than cacti do not need such extreme conditions, many of them such as certain *Echeverias* and *Kalanchoes* actually flower in the middle of winter, however they will benefit from being kept slightly cooler during the winter although they will probably need a fortnightly watering.

Repotting should be carried out as seldom as possible. Only when the plant becomes so big that it is no longer possible to water it properly does it need repotting. Repotting should be done in the early spring or autumn as this is the time when the plants are least active.

High nitrate feeds should be avoided with cacti and succulents as these tend to produce growth at the expense of flowers. A well balanced feed is required with about equal proportions of nitrogen, phosphate and potassium. Most of the foliar or spray on fertilizers on the market have this mixture and are very suitable for use with all cacti and succulents other than those succulents which are covered in soft white felt.

Cactus collection

Agave
Amaryllidaceae

AGAVE victoriæ-reginæ

Agaves are some of the best known succulents, particularly because of their abundance around the shores of the mediterranean, however they are not native to this part and come from Mexico. They are also largely responsible for the myth that Cacti only flower every hundred years and then die. This has given rise to the common name of Century Plant for *Agave americana;* although they do flower slightly more frequently in the wild. Because of this and also because of the height of their flower stems they are not often found in collections in the home, but *A. americana,* makes an attractive small rosette and its variegated form *A. americana marginata* is probably the one most often found in collections. Agaves are an important crop in Mexico; *A. sisalana* produces sisal and *A. tequilana* is the source of tequila. General culture should be as given for succulents, although they will probably benefit from being placed outside on a warm patio during the summer. If you do this, keep them away from where children may fall on them as their leaves are very sharp.

Aloe variegata
Liliaceae

This is frequently called "The Partridge Breasted Aloe" on account of the markings on the underside of the leaves. It is one of the best succulents for home use since it flowers when quite young. It produces offsets quite freely which may be removed and potted up separately once they are established, however, the flowers which are produced on three year old plants do not cause the parent plant to die off. Although it grows in South Africa it will benefit from a little shade in the home and should not be placed in direct sunlight. If given too much light the leaves turn a pale purple and no flowers will be produced. The other variety commonly seen in collections is *A. aristata* which ultimately makes a handsome clump and which also flowers fairly readily.

ALOE variegata

Aporocactus flagelliformis

Cactaceae

The appearance of this Cactus has caused it to be given the name "Rats Tail Cactus". It is not as frequently found as it should be since it grows easily and flowers readily when four years old or more. It should always be grown as a hanging plant, whether in a basket or in a pot stood on top of another inverted pot. It should be kept in as dry an atmosphere as possible during the winter as it sometimes exhibits a tendency to rot back to the main stem. If rotting is observed it is best to cut off the affected part and lightly brush the cut with Benlate or a similar fungicide. The attractive flowers are produced in the early summer indoors although those with a Greenhouse may get them to flower earlier. During the winter it will also benefit from a regular light syringing of the stems with water to prevent shrivelling and to minimise the risk of red spider mite.

APOROCACTUS flagelliformis

Astrophytum myriostigma

ASTROPHYTUM myriostigma

Cactaceae

Although the most commonly seen variety of Astrophytum, this is by no means the only one. It is easily recognised by its complete absence of spines, by the white mealy dots which cover the body and by the rigidly geometrical appearance of the ribs which has given rise to the name of Bishops Cap Cactus. There are usually five ribs but some plants may have more or less. The four sided variety is usually more square in shape with the ribs less deeply indented and has been given the name *A. myriostigma var. quadricostatum*. *A. myriostigma* may be induced to flower with little difficulty when the plants are about three years old. *A. ornatum* differs in having some spines on the ribs and in the arrangement of the mealy dots in bands on the ribs. There are hybrids between it and *A. myriostigma*. *A. asterias* is an unusual variety which should be grown grafted as a house plant since its root system is minimal and when grown in a pot there is a danger of overwatering. Both *A. ornatum* and *A. asterias* are more difficult to flower than *A. myriostigma*.

Aylostera deminuta

Cactaceae

A. deminuta is undoubtedly one of the best Cacti for the beginner. It has attractive dark green bodies which produce offsets very freely and in late Spring it is covered with fiery red flowers. It may be raised easily from seed in which case it will flower within three years of sowing. Cacti are self sterile which means that in order to produce viable seed at least two plants are required. The pollen from one should then be removed with a fine paintbrush and brushed off onto the stigma (in the centre of the flower) of the other plant. When the seed sets as a small berry it should be removed and placed in a paper envelope on a sunny windowsill. This will ripen the seeds and split the berry. The seeds should be mixed with a little dry builders sand when quite dry and then lightly sprinkled on top of some John Innes seed compost and a sheet of glass placed over the top until they have germinated. When they are big enough to handle they should be carefully pricked out. This method of seed raising applies generally to all Cacti.

AYLOSTERA deminuta

CEPHALOCEREUS senilis

Cephalocereus senilis

Cactaceae

This is the Old Man Cactus. As it is very slow growing indeed and seldom flowers under eighteen feet in height, it is grown largely for the long ornamental hairs that hang down from the areoles. In urban districts or on windowsills exposed to heavy traffic movement these long hairs may attract soot and grease which causes them to become matted: a light soaping with ordinary domestic soap will cure this problem but care must be taken to rinse the hairs properly after washing and to comb them out!

Oreocereus celsianus is frequently confused with *C. senilis* by beginners but differs in having sharp spines that prick through the hairs. *C. senilis* only has fairly small spines when young which are more like bristles.

Cereus peruvianus
Cactaceae

These are some of the best known Cacti which form densely branched candleabras in their desert habitat. The flowers are produced at night and only on older plants of about two to three feet in height. *C. peruvianus* has between four and five ribs and about six radial spines. *C. jamacaru* which is frequently incorrectly sold as *C. peruvianus* has more numerous radial spines and occasionally up to six ribs.

Two varieties of *C. peruvianus* are frequently offered for sales both of them are monstrous varieties and look as though they are deformed. In fact they will grow very well and generally make a more interesting plant than the true species. *C. peruvianus monstrosus* has much darker stems but there is also a smaller variety called *C. peruvianus monstr. minor* which adopts the monstrous appearance rather more quickly and seems to grow a little faster.

The beginner may also confuse *Myrtillocactus geometrizans* with *C. peruvianus* but the former differs in having a stout black central spine, in branching far more freely, and in having a clear line showing where the new growth has been made. *M. geometrizans* requires a slightly warmer winter temperature than other Cacti as it tends to produce brown scaly patches when too cold.

CEREUS peruvianus monstruosus

CEREUS peruvianus

CLEISTOCACTUS strausii

Cleistocactus straussii

Cactaceae

This species like most of those with a dense covering of white hair comes from the mountains. The purpose of the white hairs is to reflect away the strong sunlight in these regions and to prevent too much surface evaporation of the water in the stems. Several of the hairy Cacti grow above the snowline and in this case the hairs provide some insulation. Cacti are not frost hardy in England however since the air is too damp in winter.

C. straussii will form a clump from the base when about four to five years old, and produces flowers when two to three feet tall. The flowers are long and tubular and are produced from the side of the stem, just below the top. They hardly open at all, although the green stigma when ready for pollination protrudes from the end.

Espostoa lanata is somewhat similar in appearance but is much slower growing and is thicker near the top of the plant than the bottom. It also forms a much denser tuft of hairs near the top than *C. straussii*.

Cotyledon undulata

Crassulaceae

Although this is not an easy plant to grow well it is undeniably attractive. The scalloped leaves are borne opposite one another on the stem and have a pale waxy covering. The flowers, which are pale orange are produced at the end of the stems on long flower stalks. It is worth saving the seed of this variety as it may be raised easily following the instructions given for *Aylostera deminuta* on page 100 .

Regular spraying with a foliar fetiliser is not advised with this variety as it will damage the waxy covering and on no account should insecticides like malathion be sprayed onto the leaves. If mealy bug is found on the plant it is best to remove the bugs individually with a matchstick dipped in methylated spirits which ensures that any damage is purely local. In any event it is best not to feed it too heavily as the stems can become long and straggly and lose their graceful shape.

COTYLEDON *undulata*

CRASSULA *lycopodoides*

Crassula lycopodoides

Crassulaceae

Although not the most commonly sold Crassula, this plant is certainly one of the ones most suited to a small collection. Some pruning may be necessary to force it to form a good dense clump, but it branches quite easily. The flowers are very small indeed and are produced within the leaf axils. There is a particularly attractive variegated form, and also a variety with grey foliage.

The Crassula most commonly seen in cultivation is known as the Jade Plant and forms a small tree with jade coloured oval leaves. In the spring this produces flowers from the tips of the shoots giving it the appearance of a miniature Horse Chestnut. Although commonly sold as *C. arborescens* it is probable that many varieties of this plant are *C. portulacea* which has dark leaves seldom exceeding an inch in width. *C. arborescens* has grey leaves.

ECHEVERIA derenbergii

Echeveria

Crassulaceae

These are very popular as houseplants and a great many different varieties are grown. The original species all come from Central and South America and varieties in commercial production may be grouped under two heads; those that form rosettes such as *E. derenbergii* pictured above, which with its hybrids is the most commonly sold; and those which form a trunk on top of which the rosette is carried which are normally varieties of *E. gibbiflora*. Within the second group there is however an attractive little shrub sold sometimes as *E. harmsii* and sometimes as *Oliveranthus*

elegans. This is far more suited to the collection with limited space than the rather large *E. gibbiflora*. The rosette forming species are best grown in a shallow pan as they tend to make numerous offsets with time; the others can be grown in a conventional pot. Propagation is either by seed or by leaf cuttings; the latter is done by removing an entire leaf and laying it at a slight angle into some seed compost so that the soil just covers the severed base of the leaf. The young plant will then form at the base of the leaf.

Echinocactus grusonii

Cactaceae

This plant has been given the rather unkind name of Mother in Law's Armchair, but is more charitably often called Golden Barrell. Younger plants do not have such broad spines as the older ones and the ribs on which they are borne are more deeply notched. The yellow flowers are only produced by old plants which can attain a diameter of up to three feet in the wild.

ECHINOCACTUS grusonii

Echinocereus fitchii

Cactaceae

This plant has only recently become generally available but with its magnificent pink flowers which can be more than two inches in diameter it is an extremely worthwhile addition to a collection. It is very easily raised from seed and may even produce a few flowers within two years of sowing; it is certainly worth trying to save some seed following the instructions given under *Aylostera deminuta* on page 100 as it can rot off very easily and quite inexplicably. Ultimately it will form a handsome clump. When repotting it is better to put more peat and sand into the mixture than recommended for most cacti as it seems to prefer a more open mixture.

Several other *Echinocerei* are available on the market although frequently sold as Cereus. Notable are *E. enneacanthus* with nine spines and *E. stramineus* with wispy straw like spines. None of them flowers as readily or as profusely as *E. fitchii*.

Echinofossulocactus

syn Stenocactus

Cactaceae

This group of Cacti is distinguished by the wavy edges of the ribs and the Latin name is derived from the Greek "Echinos" meaning "Hedgehog" and the Latin "fossulatus" meaning dug out or ploughed. If you have a plant looking like a ploughed hedgehog it could be one of these. The one most commonly sold is *E. zacatecasensis* which produced white flowers tipped with pink on the top of four year old plants. *E. lancifer* has larger pink flowers produced on older plants and *E. hastatus* has yellow ones. They are all very slow growing and only need very infrequent repotting.

Euphorbia

Euphorbiaceae

EUPHORBIA mammillaris

EUPHORBIA milii

The illustrated variety is *Euphorbia milii* and this is one of the most attractive Euphorbias in cultivation. The Euphorbias, however, cover a much wider range than this, included within the genus are plants as seemingly disparate as Crotons and Poinsettias. The succulent Euphorbias range in appearance from plants like *E. trigona* (which looks like a Cereus but lacks the areoles) through shrubby varieties such as *E. milii* and *E. splendens* to the squat cylindrical varieties such as *E. obesa*.

The cactus-like upright varieties include *E. trigona* with a three ribbed stem branching freely from about nine inches upwards which is clearly variegated. *E. hermentiana* whose name is often confused with *E. trigona* has little if any variegation. Both *E. trigona* and *E. hermentiana* are fairly fast growing with small spines. *E. grandicornis* on the other hand is slower growing and normally forms a clearly marked joint after each years growth; the spines are much larger and it branches less freely. *E. resinifera* is similar in appearance to a Cereus but branches readily near the base and also lacks areoles.

The more shrubby varieties include *E. milii* (illustrated) and a larger version commonly known as *E. splendens*. Both have red flowers and sharp spines. Care should be taken when handling these varieties as some people are allergic to the white sap that flows from them. There is also a yellow variety of *E. splendens E. splendens var. Tananarive* which is sometimes seen. Another semi-shrubby but frequently prostrate variety is *E. caput medusae*, so called because the branches look like snakes. This variety is also available in a cristate form.

Spherical varieties are generally harder to find. *E. obesa* is rare, round, purple and spineless. *E. meloformis* is more common and has clearly defined ribs. There is also a probable hybrid between the two called *E. valida* which has some of the characteristics of both.

FEROCACTUS melocactiformis

Ferocactus

Cactaceae

There are many species of *Ferocactus* available on the market today but probably the most generally available is *F. wislizenii*. This in common with all the other species has vicious broad spines which are curved backwards. In Mexico where it grows wild it can become lodged in horse's hooves when young causing great pain. None of them flower until they are quite old but *F. latisinus (F. corniger)* has spines which are an attractive red colour when young, and all of them grow fairly fast and easily.

Gymnocalycium venturianum

Cactaceae

The name of this group of Cacti derives from two Greek words meaning "Naked Calyx" and refers to the complete absence of spines or bristles on the calyx of the plant. *G. quehlianum* and *G. damsii* are both fairly easy to obtain and both flower readily. *G. multiflorum* in spite of its name does not flower so readily. *G. mihanovichii* has attractive greenish flowers and has white bands on the side of the plants. Quite a lot of "Hibotan" varieties of *G. mihanovichii* are in circulation. These are almost invariably grafted and the most typical one looks like a red strawberry perched on top of a green stem. To obtain these plants the chlorophyll production has been checked in favour of other pigments. Four colours are available, red, yellow, pink and white. *G. venturianum* (illustrated) has red flowers, and *G. saglione* has attractive reddish spines but has to be much older to flower.

GYMNOCALYCIUM venturianum

Hamatocactus setispinus

Cactaceae

HAMATOCACTUS setispinus

This is deservedly one of the most popular species of Cactus, since it is easy to flower and the flowers are followed by bright red berries from which it is very easy to raise fresh plants by following the instructions given for seed raising in the section on Aylostera on page 100 . *H. setispinus* has three central spines and there is a similar species *H. hamatacanthus* which has four central spines. Although most books state that both species have a red throat so much cross hybridisation has occurred that varieties are regularly sold in the shops without this characteristic.

HAWORTHIA margaritifera

Haworthia

Liliaceae

Haworthias may at first sight be mistaken for Aloes to which they are closely related. They are very rewarding plants to grow and fall into three main types. *H. margaritifera* has stemless rosettes whose leaves are covered with white tubercles. *H. reinwardtii* bears its leaves on long stems and ultimately forms an attractive clump, while *H. cuspidata* has transparent window like flecks on the upper surfaces of the leaves. Although otherwise undemanding in their requirements Haworthias need a rest from midsummer through to mid-autumn. They should like Aloes be kept out of strong sunlight and they can be readily propagated by detaching some of the side rosettes and rooting them.

Lithops
Aizoaceae

These are well known plants which have developed in such a way as to blend perfectly with their surroundings. In contrast to their inconspicuous plant bodies the flowers are large and colourful, rather like an overgrown daisy. There are a very large number of different species and to differentiate between them would go beyond the scope of the present volume. *Lithops* require similar treatment to cacti. Their growing period starts in late spring and watering should continue until mid winter when the plants will need a complete rest and a cool environment in which to build up reserves for growth the following year.

Lobivia famatimensis
Cactaceae

The Latin name of this species is an anagram of Bolivia, the country where most of them are found. They make worthwhile additions to a collection since they are variable in flower colour and comparatively easy to grow. They look like rather overgrown *Rebutias* and need similar treatment and the flowers come out of the side of the stem from rather woolly buds. *L. famatimensis (L. densispina)* is the most commonly sold variety and due to extensive hybridisation a wide range of form are available. *L. jajoiana* invariably has red flowers which are produced nearer the top of the stem than in *L. famatimensis*, it also differs in the number of ribs; *L. famatimensis* has 12 to 15 ribs while *L. jajoiana* has 20 or more. *Pseudolobivia kratochvilleana* has trumpet shaped flowers, normally white, but occasionally flushed with pink, which are borne on long stems and *P. aurea* which is sometimes sold as *L. aurea* has yellow large flowers borne on shorter stems.

MAMMILLARIA zeilmanniana

Mammillaria
Cactaceae

The Mammillarias are best divided into two halves for descriptive purposes; those with a watery sap and those with a milky sap. Of those with a watery sap. *M. zeilmanniana* is probably the most common. It is also one of the plants most susceptible to any form of disease in the soil and rot can very quickly spread through a collection of them. For this reason it is advisable to separate some of the offsets produced each year and pot them up separately so that you always have a spare one if the big one goes wrong. *M. elongata* is frequently seen and forms a low clump with upright almost cylindrical stumps. *M. microhelia* has the spines arranged in a neat circle giving it the appearance of a sun surrounded by rays. *M. schiedeana* has rather long thin tubercles, is not very common and does better when grafted as does *M. plumosa,* one of the most beautiful of all cacti where the spines have taken on the appearance of feathers. *M. prolifera* is a good variety and quickly forms a large clump, for this reason it is best grown in a shallow pan, and *M. decipiens* and *M. camptotricha* are both similar clump forming varieties but have rather sparse long brittle spines. *M. camptotricha* has the longer spines but is the more reluctant to flower. *M. bocasana* which has hooked central spines surrounded by grey hair is a good plant for the beginner and the somewhat insignificant whitish flowers buried amongst the hairs are followed by long pink seed pods. *M.*

wildii is an excellent variety with white flowers which will tolerate a little more warmth in winter than most cacti without this having a bad effect on flower production.

The most typical of the Mammillarias with a milky sap is *M centricirrha* sometimes known as *M. magnimamma,* which has very prominent tubercles and large central spines which vary considerably from one variety to another. The flowers are only produced on older plants and are preceded by dense tufts of whitish hair which are extruded between the tubercles. *M. heyderi* is a more rewarding species for the amateur, although not very easy to obtain. The radial spines make an attractive rayed pattern and the flowers which are produced early in the year are greenish white. The plant has much more vicious spines than at first appears and care should be taken when repotting.

M. celsiana has greyish green plant bodies and produces a great deal of wool between the areoles. Even more wool is produced by *M. hahniana* which differs in having mid-green plant bodies underneath all the wool. *M. compressa,* as its name suggests looks as though someone had trodden on it, and *M. parkinsonii* which is another fairly woolly one is distinctive on account of its club shaped growth, making it look a little like an inverted pear.

Notocactus leninghaussii
Cactaceae

This cactus is deservedly popular on account of its covering of golden spines but unfortunately is a rather shy flowerer, producing flowers only in any quantity once it is about eight or nine inches in height. Some care needs to be taken when growing it, since if it grows too fast it can split open and leave a great gash in the side. If this should happen it is best to cut the unaffected top of the plant off and root it. If your plant does flower it is worth saving the seed since it is one of the easiest of all Cacti to raise in this way provided the seed is fresh. When it does flower, it normally does so in great abundance which makes the long wait worthwhile. Of the Notocacti available generally it is unusual in being a shy flowerer, the flowering ones are discussed in more detail under *N. tabularis.*

NOTOCACTUS leninghausii

Notocactus tabularis
Cactaceae

NOTOCACTUS haselbergii

N. tabularis is one of a very similar group of Cacti comprising *N. apricus* *N. muricatus,* and *N. concinnus* as well which all have smallish round bodies slightly depressed on top with short brownish spines. The number of radial spines can give a rough guide to identification as follows: 10-15 *N. concinnus;* 16-18 *N. tabularis* or *N. muricatus;* 18-20 *N. apricus* or *N. muricatus. N. muricatus* is distinguished from *N. tabularis* and *N. apricus* by having definitely brown radial spines whereas N. *tabularis* has yellow ones and *N. apricus* has yellow ones tinged with red. The same colouring applies to the central spines.

Amongst the other Notocacti are *N. ottonis* which has mid-green plant bodies with somewhat distant areoles and which forms an attractive clump round the base, and *N. submammulosus var. pampeanus* where the spines are close but flattened all round the body.

Notocacti flower only with bright sunshine and unfortunately the individual flowers do not last very long, sometimes only a matter of an hour or two at midday. It is essential to rest them thoroughly following the instructions given for general culture most carefully. As the plants start growing in the spring the dense cluster of areoles in the top of the plant open up a little and it is normally possible by mid-april to see whether any of the areoles are showing a rather more dense filling of wool than the others, and it is this that indicates the presence of a bud.

Brasilopuntia brasiliensis

Cactaceae

The Prickly Pear Family of which this species is a typical member must be one of the best known ones in the world, it was also one of the first to be described scientifically. The name is derived from a Town in Greece and it seems that the plants which are so familiar to visitors to the Mediterranean (but which are not in fact natives there) were naturalised a long time ago. Goethe also took an interest in this species and went to some trouble to raise and describe seedlings. *O. microdasys* is typical of those with short spines; the bristles that come away in your finger if you touch the plant are called glochids and may be removed either by scrubbing with soap and water or by using a glue like copydex which forms a rubbery skin on the finger and then rolling them off. *O. microdasys albispina* has white glochids and *O. microdasys rufida* has reddish ones. There is a dwarf variety of the latter named *O. microdasys rufida minor*, and a putative hybrid between *O. microdasys* and the reportedly semi-hardy *O. cantabrigiensis* called *O. x puberula*.

The Opuntia family can be broadly divided into plants with flat pads and plants with round stems; they are all characterised by the presence of glochids. Other commonly seen flat varieties are *Brasilopuntia brasiliensis (O. brasiliensis)* which has rather small light green pads, *O. leucotricha* which has oblong dark green pads with white glochids and long white hairs, and *N. coccinellifera* which is distinguished by a complete absence of spines. This last species is easy to grow and is curious in that it is the host plant for the cochineal scale insect. The species found round the Mediterranean is *O. bergeriana* and the species with edible fruits is *O. ficus-indica*.

BRASILOPUNTIA brasiliensis

Opuntia cylindrica

Cactaceae

The cylindrical Opuntias have all had their names recently changed to distinguish them from the flat ones although many growers with large stocks of old labels have not bothered to change them. The current name for *O. cylindrica* is *Austrocylindropuntia cylindrica* and it makes an attractive upright clump forming plant whose stems have a light covering of white wool. The rudimentary leaves which are formed on *A. cylindrica* fall in winter but *A. vestita* which is similar but with a more dense covering of wool has rather more persistent ones which may last the whole year. *A. salmiana* should be a must for every collection, it has narrow tubular stems and an attractive rose-like flower which is produced even on quite young plants, a feature unusual in this family.

Pterocactus tuberosus is an unusual plant and when grown on its own produces a tuber and numerous prostrate branches, it is a collectors item and is normally grown as a grafted plant in a pot unless there is really first class drainage available.

Parodia aureispina

Cactaceae

Parodias are excellent plants for the collection since a good selection of the different species can furnish flowers from March right through until the resting period sets in late September. The first to flower is *P. chrysacantha* which has long golden bristles and small trumpet shaped flowers at the top of the plant amongst them. This is closely followed by *P. aureispina* and *P. mutabilis* the former species being distinguished by the absence of red in its spines which are pure yellow. *P. sanguiniflora* follows with bright red flowers and this is turn may be followed by *P. rubellihamata* also with red flowers. *P. maïranana* and *P. gracilis* round off the season producing a long succession of orange flowers well into the autumn. Unfortunately Parodias are immensely difficult to raise from seed making them relatively unattractive for the commercial grower and this has had the effect in the past of restricting their availability.

PARODIA aureispina

Rebutia

Cactaceae

Extensive hybridisation between the various species has meant that in practice only two varieties of Rebutia which are commercially available can be distinguished. Those with very white spines or bristles are probably related to *R. senilis* while those without are generally related to *R. minuscula, R. deminuta* or *R. violaciflora*. Water should not be given to any of the Rebutias in the spring until the red flower buds round the base of the plant are at least one-tenth of an inch long, otherwise they may fall off and fresh plant bodies develop.

REBUTIA spp

Rhipsalidopsis rosea

Cactaceae

This plant is becoming increasingly available and flowers during the early spring. It needs slightly more warmth than normal Cacti during the winter and will consequently also require a little water. Great care must be taken with watering, however, as it is very susceptible to overwatering.

Schlumbergera gaertneri

Cactaceae

SCHLUMBERGERA gaertneri

This is probably the most easily obtainable of all the "leaf Cacti" where the stems have been replaced by flattened leaf like joints. It is commonly known as the Whitsun Cactus in contrast to *Zygocactus truncatus* (qv) known as the Christmas Cactus. *S. gaertneri* is fairly tolerant of adverse conditions and is best put outside during the summer so that the pads may ripen sufficiently to form buds. Watering should commence as soon as the red pips are visible at the tips of the stems, and it is these red pips that subsequently become the flower buds.

114

SEDUM pachyphyllum   *SEDUM rubrotinctum*

Sedum

Crassulaceae

Many Sedums are almost completely hardy in England, such as *S. acre, S. rosea* and *S. anglicum.* These make excellent plants for a rock-garden and along with *Sempervivums* and the curious *Orostachys spinosus* from the Far East can provide an excellent link between a Cactus collection and a conventional garden. Of the non-hardy species one of the best is *S. sieboldii variegatum* which can also be grown as a hanging basket. The leaves are greyish with a large cream coloured blotch in the middle and it produces pink flowers on long stems in the autumn. *S. lineare variegatum* has thin leaves edged with white, is rather more delicate than the preceding species and rather more difficult to flower. Another commonly seen *Sedum* is *S. pachyphyllum* aptly named as "Jelly Beans" which it uncannily closely resembles. In common with most other Crassulas great care should be taken before using insecticides such as Malathion since they can suffer from an application. As with all fertilisers and insecticides the instructions for use should be read carefully first.

Setiechinopsis mirabilis

Cactaceae

This fascinating plant is one of the easiest of the nocturnal flowering species to flower. The flowers only last about one night and are at their best about nine-o-clock in the evening when it is just possible to catch the faint scent they give off. They are pure white and are borne at the end of long stems rising from the top of the plant. The plant is a difficult one to grow to any size and since it sets seed readily it is best to save and propagate the seeds using the method given under *Aylostera deminuta.*

Stapelia
Asclepiadaceae

These curious plants are easily distinguished by
the enormous star-fish like flowers that are
produced near the base of the stem and hang over
the side of the pot. One of the most spectacular is
S. gigantea which lives up to its name with flowers
14 inches in diameter. If you can be present as the
buds open you will hear a faint but quite audible
explosion as the flower emerges. *S. variegata* is the
commonest of the species in cultivation and has
sinister blotched leopard-like flowers and greyish
green stems. *Stapelias* have small root systems and
are therefore best grown in pans if possible which
allow them to form large clumps without
encumbering them with too much soil. They need
a minimum winter temperature of 45°F and also
some shade during the summer months. Although
they can be raised from seed it is easier and faster
to take cuttings.

A closely related plant which is frequently seen in
collections is *Ceropegia woodii*, which is a
climbing plant with heart-shaped blotched purple
leaves and tubers which are produced at the nodes
of the stems.

STAPELIA

ZYGOCACTUS truncatus

Zygocactus truncatus
Cactaceae

These are easily grown on windowsills and make a
most attractive display at Christmas. Culture is
fairly straightforward. The main growing period is
during the summer and early autumn when they
should be watered just like any other houseplant.
Towards the end of the summer, however, they
will need a position with plenty of light in order to
assist in bud formation. A couple of month's resting period should then follow in a cooler spot such
as a bedroom windowsill, and then watering
should start a few weeks before Christmas. After
the plants have finished flowering they will need
another short rest for three or four weeks before
growth starts up again. Although the commonest
variety has pink flowers, there is an attractive
orange flowered variety called "Weihnach-
stfreude."

FLOWERING PLANTS FROM BULBS

There is little to match a number of the plants grown from bulbs for ease of culture and showy flowers. Several of these subjects are not only colourful but very sweetly scented. Good results are assured as long as the simple and straightforward cultural instructions are followed to the letter. The greater the difference in flowering time from the normal, the more important it is to strictly follow the instructions.

CROCUS vernus 'Purpureus Grandiflorus'

CROCUS vernus 'Joan of Arc'

Crocus

There are three main groups of *Crocus*, the autumn flowering one which produces flowers before the leaves in September, the February flowering *Crocus* species which has smaller flowers than the best known and largest flowering "Dutch Crocus". Whilst all three can be flowered in pots indoors the last group is most suited to indoor decoration. The corms should be planted in the autumn and left either outside or indoors in very cool conditions (10°C, 50°F and less) until the shoots are well developed, the tips of the leaves showing and the plump flower bud just visible. At this point they can be brought into warmer conditions, 15°C (60°F) and a light position where the buds will quickly develop and flower. Bring into warm conditions too soon and the leaves grow away rapidly and the flower bud withers. Watch out for mice when the corms are planted and developing roots and shoots, at this stage they are a tempting rodent delicacy.

The John Innes composts, either seed or potting, are ideal for *Crocus* and flowered plants can be planted in the garden to produce more colour in future years. If you are using the special crocus bowls with holes around the side, planting up is made easier by waiting until the crocus have developed shoots 1 cm long. The shoots can then be placed through the holes while potting up. Most of these crocus bowls have no drainage holes in the base and care should be taken when watering to avoid waterlogging in the base of the pot.

One plant, commonly and incorrectly called "Autumn Crocus" and correctly called *Colchicum*, can be flowered by just standing on the window sill. Immediately after flowering they should be planted in the garden. The "Voodoo Lily", seen in the *Crocus* illustration top left , can also be given this treatment.

CROCUS vernus 'Yellow Mammouth'

118

Hippeastrum

There can be no more dramatic flowering bulb than the *Hippeastrum* hybrids, often sold under the common name "Amaryllis". The larger the bulb you buy, the more likely it is to flower and the more flower stems and flowers on the stems in the first year. Many bulbs are sold before Christmas, those sold in the autumn flower in winter and early spring, spring purchased bulbs flower in the summer. They require a pot 5 cm (2 in) larger than the diameter of the bulb and any compost to the strength of John Innes Potting Compost No. 2, the bulb half covered with compost.

Once potted they need warmth from the base, 20°C (70°F). Stand the pot on a shelf over a radiator to get roots and shoots growing quickly, then move to cooler, normal room conditions, 13-15°C (55°-60°F) and a light position. The flower shoot often precedes the leaves and once growth starts treat as for ordinary house plants. After flowering continue to water and give a fortnightly liquid feed. It is possible to keep the leaves throughout the year, maintaining the watering and feeding. It is preferable, in my opinion, to reduce and then stop watering several months after flowering, dry the bulbs off and rest for three months before starting into growth again, either in late autumn or early spring.

Do not repot annually, these bulbs thrive under restricted root conditions and a good baking in the sun when watering ceases improves the flowering potential. New plants are obtained by detaching offsets from mature plants when repotting, every third or fourth year.

This really is a most spectacular flower and is especially useful to brighten the window sills and groups of house plants in early spring.

HIPPEASTRUM hybrid, a few weeks from planting

Close up of hybrid flowers

HYACINTHUS orientalis 'Delft Blue'

HYACINTHUS orientalis 'Jan Bos'

Hyacinthus

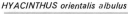

HYACINTHUS orientalis albulus

The dense flower spikes and heady fragrance of the "Dutch Hyacinth" are the cream of all bulb flowers. Some people may prefer the very early, smaller and more delicate "Roman Hyacinths". We have the choice for indoor culture of either prepared or ordinary bulbs. The prepared bulbs are lifted just as soon as possible, put into stores and held at a high temperature to convince the bulbs they have had their concentrated summer then subjected to a lower temperature to imitate a concentrated autumn. When we buy them in September the bulbs think it is mid winter! If potted at once and given a couple more months in the cool to develop roots and a shoot 4-6 cm high they can then be brought indoors, placed in a light position and warm temperature, up to 20°C (70°F) to flower at Christmas.

The ordinary unprepared bulbs can be brought into flower much earlier than normal by potting up in September and October and bringing indoors in December/February to flower from January to February. The secret of successful 'Hyacinth' growing is to give plenty of cool growing time for root and shoot development. If the flower shoot is 6 cm high, be sure to wait too long rather than not long enough for shoot growth, warmth can be given and the spikes soon develop.

Iris

The small bulbous *Iris* makes some of the most charming subjects for early spring flowering indoors. It is wise to avoid the larger flowering "Dutch, Spanish and English Iris", which require very careful cultivation for satisfactory flowering indoors in pots. Three dwarf species, *Iris danfordiae* with clear yellow flowers, *Iris histrioides* with Oxford blue flowers and *Iris reticulata* with deep violet flowers are the best for pots and bowls, growing no more than 12 cm high. The sweet fragrance of *I. danfordiae* and violet-like fragrance of *I. reticulata* are specially recommended.

There are several cultivars of *Iris reticulata* like the pale blue *I. r.* 'Cantab', all of which are suited to pot culture. Plant these bulbs in pots and pans filled with John Innes Potting Compost No. 1 and treat as for *Crocus*, being sure to leave the pans outside in the cold until flower buds show colour. The bulbs are perfectly hardy and are equally attractive in the rock garden pushing through the snow. Bulbs which have flowered indoors can subsequently be planted in the garden.

A few 7 cm pots filled with these delightful plants can be used to great effect in a bowl arrangement of house plants. In this association they provide flower colour and fragrance in the depths of winter. If you have such a bowl arrangement the flowering miniature *Iris* can be followed by either *Primula acaulis* or *Scilla*.

IRIS reticulata 'Clairette'

IRIS dandfordiae

LILIUM 'Enchantment'   LILIUM 'Destiny'

Lilium

Exotic and colourful flowers, strong fragrance and bulbs which, after flowering, can be planted in the garden to flower again in future years are but some of the qualities offered by Lily bulbs. An extensive hybridisation programme in recent years, especially by the Oregon Bulb Farm of Jan de Graff, has brought a whole range of exciting new forms which are easy to grow and very attractive.

Bulbs of both *Lilium longiflorum* and the Mid Century Hybrids, including *L.* 'Cinnabar', *L.* 'Destiny' and *L.* 'Enchantment', can be stored in the refrigerator at 4-7°C (40-45°F) and by careful manipulation of light and heat brought into flower at any time of the year.

Under normal home and garden conditions the easiest way is to grow to the natural season, bringing the plants into flower a few weeks earlier with the warmer indoor temperature. The Mid Century Hybrids are most strongly recommend and bulbs 10-12 cm in circumference should be potted one to a 13 cm (5 in) pot and three to a 20-24 cm (8-10 in) pot in the winter. Set the bulb deep in the pot because most of the lilies are stem rooting and as the shoot emerges roots are formed on the new stem. While more flowers are carried by bulbs grown in peat and sand compost the best overall results are obtained with the soil based John Innes No. 1 potting compost.

A cool period, ideally with the temperature at 2°C (35°F), should be given before bringing indoors into a temperature of 15°C (60°F) and a light position from early January onwards. Bring in one or more pots per week for several weeks to get a succession of flowering plants. The bulbs started into growth in early January will be in flower in early April. Feeding is not required where the soil based compost is used.

If you have the space, in say a sun lounge or glass lined porch, some of the taller summer flowering lilies can be grown. Really exotic flowers are produced by *Lilium auratum* and *Lilium speciosum* cultivars. For very heavy perfume in June/July indoors try growing a few bulbs of *Lilium regale*, it is a very easy plant to grow in pots.

Be sure all the lilies have a light position, especially those plants started into growth in mid winter when the days are short and the light poor.

LILIUM 'Cinnabar'

NARCISSUS 'Cragford'

NARCISSUS 'Golden Harvest'

Narcissus

There are few positions indoors which cannot be made more beautiful in winter and early spring with either a pot or bowl of flowering "Daffodils". Botanically we list all the plants under the generic name *Narcissus* but most people make a common distinction by referring to the large trumpet flowers as "Daffodils" and the small cup flowers as "Narcissi".

They are all beautiful, from the tiny 8-10 cm high miniatures like "Angels Tears", *Narcissus triandus albus,* to the real giant trumpet flowers of cultivars like *N.* 'Dutch Master'. The range of flower form and colour is ever increasing and it is well worth ringing the changes by planting up a few pots of the more recent and unusual flower colours from lime green to tangerine orange and scarlet.

The potting composts, preferably John Innes No. 1, are ideal growing mediums and containers with drainage holes are best if you wish to grow the plants on after flowering to rebuild the strength of the bulbs and subsequently plant in the garden to flower in future seasons. If you plant in shallow bowls give the maximum area of compost for root development by covering the bulbs by no more than half, even if this means providing cane and twine support for the leaves and flowers.

One very good tip to get maximum flowers from a given container is to plant two layers. For example, take a 15 cm (6 in) flower pot, half fill it with compost and plant as many bulbs in this first layer as the space allows. Add some more compost and then plant a second layer of bulbs in the usual

way on the top before finally filling with compost. The lower layer grows and catches up with the top one to give double the number of flowers in any one pot. If you require a long period of flowering rather than a mass, choose early and late flowering cultivars.

Once again, the secret of successful culture is patience, pot up the bulbs as soon as possible in the autumn and leave in the cool and dark for roots and shoots to develop. Placing outside against a north facing wall and covering with peat is one good way to do this and you can also place in a black polythene bag in a cool shed or room. See that the bag is inflated sufficiently and the top tied to prevent the sides of the bag from rubbing against the emerging leaves and causing brown tips. When the leaves have grown sufficiently to show the flower bud clearly the bowls can be brought into the light and slowly into warmer conditions to force them into early flowering. Once the flower bud is clear of the neck of the bulb the temperature can be raised from 10°C (50°F) to 20°C (70°F) but at the higher temperature, especially if associated with dark room conditions, the leaves and flower stems are long, drawn and weak.

Daffodil bulbs can be grown in bowls filled with pebbles and water, this is an interesting thing for children to do and one of the best varieties for this water culture is *N.* 'Cragford', as the illustration clearly indicates. If you really want fragrance then the multi-headed flower stemmed cultivars like *N.* 'Cragford' and *N.* 'Geranium' should be chosen.

Scilla

Another group of small flowering bulbous plants ideal for bowl culture is the *Scilla,* commonly called "Early Flowering Squill", and especially the bright blue "Siberian Squill", *S. siberica,* and the paler blue, lightly striped flowers of *S. tubergeniana.* They are grown just the same as *Hyacinthus* with the bulbs planted in pots any time in the autumn up to mid November. A period of cool conditions is needed to allow root and shoot development before bringing into the light and gentle heat 10-15°C (50-60°F) in the new year.

If you want the flowers to last as long as possible, choose *S. s.* 'Spring Beauty' growing 15 cm (6 in) high and twice the size of the species. These delphinium blue flowers are sterile and last much longer than the seed forming kinds. The rich blue flowering kinds associate well with the smaller flowered yellow specii *Crocus* and the yellow and cream shades of *Primula acaulis.*

These plants are equally attractive grown in outdoor containers like window boxes, hanging baskets and troughs as well as the obvious setting in the rock garden with yellow "Aconites". Their natural flowering season is February and March and with a little warmth they can be flowered indoors in January.

SCILLA tubergeniana

Single early Tulips

Tulipa

Great care is required in the selection of varieties and the cultural conditions provided for tulips grown to flower at Christmas. It may be wise to wait a little longer for the flowers and have a wider choice of variety and less demanding growing conditions. For Christmas flowering select varieties like *T.* 'Brilliant Star Maximus', scarlet, *T.* 'Mignon', a deliciously scented pink, and *T.* 'Golden Ducat' a double golden yellow. Plant them in pots and bowls by mid September, plunge in either peat or soil and keep very cool, watering if necessary to help reduce temperature. Bring the bowls indoors on the last day or two of November to a temperature of 18°C (65°F) and keep them dark. When the shoots have grown another 3-5 cm move to the light and raise the temperature to 20°C (70°F).

February and March flowering is much easier to cope with indoors. The early flowering tulips are best and include the Single and Double Earlies, the Mendels and some Specie Hybrids. For later flowering, but still ahead of outdoor planted bulbs, the Triumph and Darwin Tulips should be chosen. After planting either plunge or keep in cool dark conditions for 10-12 weeks, by which time the roots should be well established and the shoots 6-8 cm high. At this stage bring the bowls into a temperature of 12-15°C (55-60°F) but keep them dark to lengthen the stem for 10 to 14 days. Gradually expose to full light, place a sheet of newspaper over the bowls to achieve this gradual lighting process, and avoid bottom heat and extremes of temperature.

A good tip for successful tulip culture in pots is never to bring the bowls in until mid January at the earliest and not before the shoots are 9 cm high.

125

Zantedeschia

Whilst not strictly speaking a pot plant for the home, *Zantedeschia aethiopica* does grow very well in 20-25 cm (8-10 in) pots and is a good subject for the sun lounge and glass-sided home extension. In mild areas this plant will survive outside and is therefore a likely plant for the cool greenhouse and unheated room.

The fleshy rootstock is divided and repotted in early autumn, using either John Innes No. 2 or the proprietary peat composts for potting. Plant the roots 6-8 cm. deep and keep the compost just moist until growth commences. Then increase the watering as growth increases until in full growth and flower, when heavy watering is required. In fact the cultivar Z. *a.* 'Crowborough' can be grown out of doors as an aquatic in a water depth of 24-48 cm (6-12 in) and, incidently, is one of the most hardy forms available. A weekly liquid feed is also advisable from early February to April.

If you are tempted to cut the flowers from your pot grown plants avoid cutting leaves which build up the rootstock and produce the food reserves for next year's flowering. There are forms with green flowers and others with white spotted leaves, qualities sought by the modern floral arranger. These plants are not freely available but are worth seeking out.

Once flowering has finished, that is in late spring, early summer, reduce watering and allow the plants to dry off. While these plants are evergreen it is easiest to dry them off leaving the filled pots on their sides until September/October when the compost should be renewed and the plants started into growth again.

Provide as much light as possible during the winter and early spring, a sunny south window at the least. If you have finished with the plants indoors and wish to establish them in the garden, protect the crowns from frost with 20-24 cm of either dry peat or straw through the winter.

Enjoy your plants more

The following pages describe how

The pleasing effect of the mixed bowl arrangement.

Plants thrive
in their own humid atmosphere

Glass and clear plastic containers are perfect for plants and attractive small plant collections and indoor gardens can be planted up in the larger containers. Plants in these containers are in a naturally more humid atmosphere away from draughts and dust. It should be remembered, however, that where tinted glass, like big glass bottles, is used light is reduced and shade-loving plants like ferns should be used.

When planting up a large bottle make a long paper tube to funnel in the compost which should be of John Innes Potting Compost No. 1 strength. Avoid flowering plants in containers which have a narrow neck because it is difficult to remove the dead flowers. Where condensation occurs over the inside of a glass container and obstructs vision, open it up until the glass dries and then seal again. It may be necessary to do this several times before the moisture level reaches equilibrium and the container can remain sealed.

Plants for your home

The quality of life for each one of us can be improved by the presence of well grown indoor plants. Beauty of leaf, flower and fruit attracts the eye and the fragrance of many plants refreshes and lightens the spirit. We work and relax more effectively in attractive surroundings and growing plants provide instant embellishment to the most dismal decor. Dry atmospheres caused by central heating can also be corrected by the use of living plants.

Whilst the title and theme of this book is Plants for your Home, the value of plants indoors goes much further than this. The decoration and improvement of all commercial premises, reception and work areas is possible with the right selection of plants.

The range is vast and we have a choice for every situation in home and office. A casual glance at plants on window sills, filing cabinets, troughs and containers clearly indicates the natural love we all have for plants indoors. They are easy to grow and this book has as its objective the improvement in plant quality indoors and the increase in pleasure to be gained from growing plants.

Care
of house plants

There are five basic elements which control the growth and health of plants, both indoors and in the garden. If plants are to grow at all they need air, light, warmth — and sometimes a period of cool, so this factor might be better described as temperature — water and a rooting medium which usually contains plant food. All five are easily provided in the right proportions in the home, although certain styles of living room accommodation are more suited to certain plants.

AIR

Taking each element in its turn, air is by far the easiest, with plenty available in every situation.

The only qualification might be pollution of the air and the fact that *town* gas produces fumes which damage plants is well known. Fortunately town gas has now given way to natural gas which, far from damaging plants, actually enriches the atmosphere with carbon dioxide and improves plant growth.

The only other references to air in house plant care terms are the need to provide a buoyant atmosphere for some plants, which really means fresh air and air change without draughts, and to provide a humid atmosphere which relates to moisture content and watering.

Select the right plants for the situation,
the sunlovers in full sun and the plants that thrive in shade at the furthest point from the light source.

LIGHT

Air is easy, you just use what there is and light comes into the same category, although here we exercise some choice in the plants' interest. Strong light in mid-summer is too hot and bright for many plants standing on window sills exposed to the midday sun. Fortunately we do not want all plants standing on the sunny side of the home and many plants are better appreciated from all sides, which means siting in from the window.

If we measure the strength of light across a room, obviously it will be strongest at the window, with a gradual fall off in strength the further we move away. There are three degrees of light strength in house plant growing terms, *strong direct* light — on and around the window sill, *indirect* light — in a bit from the glass, up to 2 metres (6 feet) from the average house window but still a light position, and *shaded* positions well away from the window. There are the very shaded positions in which it is too dark for most of us to read, and here even the most shade-loving subjects will require a regular period of recuperation in a light position. The alternative is to choose from a few plants which will grow in artificial light. Such artificial lighting means a light bulb or tube within one and a half metres (4½ ft) switched on for twelve to sixteen hours a day. The *Saintpaulia* is a good example of a plant which will grow under this kind of artificial light.

While the three degrees of light strength are easily understood we must also remember that the light is much stronger in summer than in winter. This usually means moving a plant up one in the light stakes as winter approaches. For example, the *Cyclamen*, quite happy in an indirectly lit position in the summer will be better in direct light in winter. The *Chlorophytum, Cissus* and *Hedera*, growing happily in shaded positions in summer will grow better if moved to a brighter, indirectly lit position in the winter.

Insufficient light is evident by thin, long growth, that is thin stems, wide spaces between the leaves, pale colour of young leaves and growing tips. Leaves of plants brought into a new position which is too dark quickly turn yellow.

WATER

The introduction of central heating, whilst providing a steady warm temperature in winter, which suits many house plants, dries out the atmosphere. This dry atmosphere is not ideal for either human beings or most house plants.

Sophisticated air conditioning systems hold humidity at 40-50%. without such control most of us need to make efforts to increase the moisture content of the centrally heated room, especially in winter. The introduction of house plants naturally increases humidity and for those plants which require additional moisture in the air, there are several ways of meeting their needs.

The best method of doing this is to stand the pot in a bowl filled with damp peat. Select the lighter coloured peats, thoroughly soak them in water, gently squeeze out some of the water and allow to drain before packing round the pot, which has been stood in a larger bowl. There are several variations on this theme, including filling a pot plant saucer with shingle or pebbles, standing the pot on the pebbles and keeping the pebbles damp. Alternatively, use a block of wood in the water-filled saucer and stand the pot on this.

A group of plants will provide their own micro-climate and if a peat-filled-bowl plunged plant is in the centre of a group it will give additional moisture in the immediate vicinity. The use of a cheap syringe which allows the leaves to be sprayed with clear water every day or so is a great help.

A block of wood in a saucer of water helps to provide humidity round the plant. Porous clay pots absorb more water and create a damper atmosphere than plastic.

Provision of a humid atmosphere is of lesser importance than the actual watering. Overwatering and underwatering account more than anything else for the rapid loss of 'shine' and vigorous healthy growing appearance we require from our indoor plants. We need to imitate nature for most indoor plants and provide water (like rain), allow this to dry out somewhat (the effect of a sunny period) before watering again, not keep constantly wet or constantly dry.

If you have difficulty in assessing the water requirement of plants, try the silver sand-filled saucer system. This helps increase humidity and does the watering in a way which imitates a commercial grower system. After filling the saucer, thoroughly wet the sand and stand the pot plant on the sand, giving the pot a slight twist to ensure that sand and compost in the base of the pot are in contact. Then water the pot plant once from the top. The water trickles through the compost and when it reaches the sand it completes the moisture contact and water flows up into the compost by capillary attraction. All you need to do from this point is to keep the sand damp all the time. It couldn't be easier, the plant draws up the moisture it needs and the compost remains just nicely damp.

This sand system may provide too much moisture in the winter for a few plants. Here an alternative system is to check the weight.

When the compost is nicely moist the compost will be much heavier than when it is dry. If you watch nurserymen you will see them lift plants to check whether watering is required and all they are doing is feeling the weight. If you have not enough experience to assess the difference in weight, scales can be used for the smaller specimens. When you purchase your plant, ask the skilled sales person whether the compost is damp enough. Once you are home, weigh the plant and write the weight on the side of the pot. The compost will dry and as it does the weight will become less and once 30-40 gm (1-2 oz) are lost from a 9 cm (3½ in) pot, add water until the original weight is achieved. There will be a proportionally larger difference for larger pots.

When the winter comes, the day length and light strength is at its lowest, growth slows down and less water is required. This is the time to put most plants on a weight watchers diet and reduce the amount of water given and the amount of moisture in the compost. The water requirement for each plant is described in the descriptive section and while, for example, *Ficus* is a winter weight watcher, the "Cineraria" *(Senecio)* and *Primula* will be happy on their saucers of damp sand.

Many foliage plants can be kept smaller and more compact by reducing the water given to them by a third. The only practical way of measuring this third is the weight watering scheme.

These two watering systems may be too precise for the casual house plant grower and regular attention to watering is all that is required. When the compost is almost dry, water well and then leave well alone until the compost is almost dry again, that is all the plant requires to thrive.

Automatic watering is achieved by standing the pot on a saucer filled with damp silver sand. Water the plant once from the top to start off the water uptake.

Watering by weight, check the weight of a plant when nicely moist, record this weight and when the compost dries by 30-40 grams (1-2 oz), add water until back to original weight.

Rainwater is ideal for all plants and ordinary tap water quite acceptable for the majority. Plants which do not like lime and for which rainwater is not available should be watered with the condensate from the refrigerator. Another method of reducing the alkalinity of tap water for ericaceous plants is to place an old stocking filled with light coloured sphagnum peat in a container of water for a day or, then use this water for plants. The perennial question how often to water is a teaser, less in winter than in summer and more often in high than low temperatures, is the only sensible answer.

Sand, loam and peat are the basic ingredients in the majority of house plant composts.

TEMPERATURE

The temperature requirements of different plants varies tremendously and in this book we have attempted to provide an accurate guide to the minima required by plants for survival in a reasonable condition. Some plants are hardy and will stand frost, others are really tender hot-house subjects. The one general rule to observe when growing plants at the lower levels of their temperature requirement is to be sparing with the water.

Plants in situations with inadequate light are better at lower temperature levels, warm conditions just speed the production of thin, drawn and spindly growth. When tender plants are purchased during the winter, avoid exposing them to really cold conditions and harsh drying winds during the journey home.

When siting plants indoors avoid draughty positions, not just cold draughts from the window but desiccating air movement above radiators, close to the hot air heater or air conditioning outlets. Many central heating systems automatically cut back the temperature late at night through to the early hours of the morning. This drop in temperature can be quite severe, especially for plants behind curtains on the window sill and isolated from the warmth within the room. Avoid this by bringing plants inside the curtains at night and, even better, site the plants on furniture close to the window but inside the curtains and not right over the radiator.

ROOTING MEDIUM — COMPOST

Most people buy proprietary compost ready mixed for house plants, but a few words on the basic constituents are of value, especially in relation to watering and feeding. There are three materials, sand, peat and loam, which form the majority of mixes. The sand needs to be acid in nature, if it contains chalk this can seriously affect the subsequent plant food supply in a variety of mixes. Fine, well washed sand is used in the peat and sand composts while a coarser grit, up to 3 mm (⅛ in) grist is used in the loam based John Innes Compost.

A wide variety of peat types are used and as a general rule the lighter coloured sphagnum peats, not too fine and of granular texture, are the best. The granulation provides good aeration in the compost. Loam (the technical word for soil) in purists' terms means virgin turf (rich soil under grass not previously used to grow other plants) cut and stacked for twelve months before chopping down and screening to remove stones.

Loam, sterilised with steam to kill weed seeds, diseases and pests, is the basis for all John Innes Composts. The J. I. Potting Composts consist of 7 parts by volume of loam: 3 parts peat: 2 parts grit. Thirty six litres (1.26 cu. ft. or 1 bushel) of compost also requires 21 gm (¾oz) ground chalk or limestone and 113 gm (4 oz) of John Innes base fertiliser for the J. I. Potting Compost No. 1. For the J. I. Potting Compost No. 2 just double the base fertiliser, for J. I. No. 3 treble it.

Peat and sand mixes are usually in the proportion 75% peat: 25% sand by volume and we also have the all-peat composts. Base fertilisers for each of these "soilless" composts contain minute quantities of trace elements and thorough mixing of fertiliser into the compost is best left to the manufacturer. The margin for error is less in the soilless composts and care should be taken not to overfeed in these mixes and to avoid the composts drying out completely. When really dry the remaining moisture in the compost can become too rich in plant food and further, rewetting of the compost can be difficult.

Where a small quantity of compost is needed in the home, by far the easiest way is to nip out and buy a bag ready mixed. The soilless composts can be stored, as long as they are kept dry, the soil based ones need using within a few months. Do not over firm the all-peat composts, the very lightest of firming is all they require.

REPOTTING AND POTTING-ON

We need compost for two operations, both almost self explanatory. *Repotting* means taking the plant from its pot, the removal of some old compost and replacement by new compost when repotting back into the same size of pot. *Potting-on* refers to taking the plant from its pot and moving up into the next one or two sizes larger pot. Another good general rule for house plants is to avoid over potting, that is moving up into too large a pot too quickly. A two-size move is invariably more than adequate, for example, moving a 9 cm (3½in) pot plant up into a 13 cm (5½ in) pot. Moving from a 9 cm (3½ in) pot to an 11 cm (4¼ in) is not too easy because there is insufficient room to get compost down between the plant root ball at the side of the pot with the fingers. The larger the pot size, however, the more room there is for the one-size up potting-on.

If you wish to check to see if the loam based compost has the right moisture content, squeeze a handful. If at the correct level, when the hand is opened the compost will just crack open, too dry and it will crumble away, too wet and it stays in a cake.

A Chlorophytum with roots absolutely filling the 9 cm (3½ in) pot ready for potting-on into a 13 cm (5½ in) pot.

All plants must be well watered before repotting.

There is an adequate range of pot sizes for all plants, the variegated ivy is in the popular 9 cm (3½ in) size. Four saucers without drainage holes can be seen in the foreground.

Two step-by-step methods of potting-on in pictorial sequence.

SYSTEM ONE

1. Clay pots with a large single drainage hole need a piece of broken crock over the hole to maintain drainage. This crocking is not required in plastic pots with several drainage holes, for soilless composts and for plants to be watered by capillarity from below, for example on a saucer of damp sand.

2. Having placed a handful or so of compost in the larger pot, remove the plant from its pot, checking that the soil ball is thoroughly moistened.

3. The old soil ball is deep enough in the new pot to be just covered when potting is complete. Start infilling compost all round the pot.

4. Firm the compost with the fingers as you go.

5. When completed there should be at least half an inch depth of pot left for watering. Check to see the compost for potting has the right moisture content.

6. The all-peat composts have the right moisture level for use if water oozes between the fingers when a handful is squeezed hard. Warm water mixes into dry peat compost more easily than cold.

 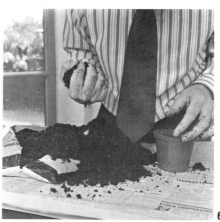

POTTING-ON SYSTEM TWO

Especially suitable for plastic pots and soilless compost.

1. Take the plant from its original pot and place the plant carefully to one side.

2. Place a handful or so of new compost in the new pot and then put the old pot in the place to be filled by the plant in due course.

3. Fill in between the two pots, gently firming as you go.

4. Remove the old pot and leave exactly the right sized hole in the right position for the plant. If the hole is not quite central, too deep or too shallow, just knock out and start again.

5. Pop the plant soil ball into the hole, give the pot a tap and gently firm to complete potting.

Seeds
Cuttings and Bulbs

The very keen indoor plant grower may wish to raise a few plants like *Thunbergia*, "Black-eyed Susan", from seed. It is necessary to loosely fill a flower pot with moistened seed compost, firm gently and then sprinkle the seed over the surface, just cover with more seed compost and water once with a fine spray from above. The pot should then be enclosed in a polythene bag and placed in a warm position. A black polythene bag is advisable unless the warm position is a well shaded one. Watch for the first signs of germination, when the bag can be removed and the pot moved to a light position. Just as soon as the seedling is large enough to handle, it can be moved into a small pot of its own, filled with potting compost of the lowest fertiliser strength.

Raising new plants from cuttings, made from the tips of growing shoots, can be a fascinating pastime, with the easiest of plants, like *Fuchsia*, *Impatiens* — "Busy Lizzie", *Rhoicissus* — "Grape Ivy" and *Tradescantia* — "Wandering Jew", rooting in a glass of water on a sunny window sill in summer. If you wish to experiment with vegetative propagation of some of the more difficult subjects then the polythene bag is needed again, this time a clear bag which lets in as much light as possible. Condensation inside the bag provides sufficient shade for all but the most tender subjects and for these the ideal is a white polythene bag.

Here, although it is possible to manage with all-peat, the best system is to use a mixture of equal parts peat and sand. Loosely fill a pot with the mixture, gently firm and sprinkle a little sand over the top. Into this we can push 5-7cm (2-3 in) long tip cuttings, cut off just below a leaf joint of those plants listed above and others, and also leaf stalks, leaves and pieces of leaves of certain plants, all of which will produce young plants from the cut surface.

Perhaps the best known leaf cutting is provided by *Saintpaulia* — "African Violet". Select a fully developed leaf, snap it off the parent plant and push the stem into the compost. In warm conditions new leaves will appear in a couple of months, the warmer the conditions the faster the growth. Similar leaf stalk cuttings are possible with *Peperomia* and even sections of the leaf cut into squares of large postage stamp size of plants like *Begonia rex* and *Streptocarpus* will root and grow.

Once these cuttings are inserted in the well moistened compost, syringe with water and cover with the polythene bag. If the bag is sealed round the rim of the pot with a rubber band no further watering will be required before the cutting starts to grow and the bag can then be removed. Dipping the cut surface of the cuttings in a proprietary rooting hormone before inserting in the compost speeds the formation of roots.

A "Grape Ivy" cutting rooted in summer in a glass of water on a sunny window sill.

The cutting is potted into compost in the same way as larger plants.

Feeding indoor plants

Freshly potted plants will have ample fertiliser in the compost to support strong growth. The larger the plant and the stronger its growth, the quicker will the reserves of plant food in the compost be exhausted. It is possible for the home gardener to make up his own John Innes base fertiliser, after all it is only a matter of mixing two parts by weight hoof and horn meal, two parts superphosphate and one part sulphate of potash.

Once the base fertiliser in the compost has been used the compost can be topped up by sprinkling some more John Innes base fertiliser on the surface and watering it in. This is a practical proposition for window boxes and the strong growing plants, for example large ivies in the bigger containers, specimen *Fuchsia* and *Pelargonium.*

Liquid fertilisers are by far the easiest and in my view the best method of feeding indoor plants, however. A few drops added to the water when watering is very easy, very rapid in its effect and totally satisfactory, both for the condition of the plant and for the chemical balance of the compost.

Between the two extremes of the newly potted plant requiring no liquid feed and the large plant in a small pot requiring a very dilute liquid feed at virtually every watering there are many variations. We can provide several rule of thumb guide-lines to follow. First, always see that the compost is just damp before watering with liquid feed. The majority of plants make most of their growth during spring, summer and early autumn and this is the time to liquid feed. The exceptions are winter flowering plants, especially the seed raised ones, which require feeding up to and part way through the flowering period, from the time there are signs of fertiliser in the compost becoming exhausted.

Excessive and inadequate feeding, like over and under-watering, are major contributors to loss of shine and poor growth. How do we tell when a plant needs more plant food? Paling of leaf colour and a slowing down in speed of growth are the two most obvious signs. When you are watching the leaves and looking for signs of the green colour lightening to indicate food reserves are running out, remember that lack of light and overwatering can have the same effect.

Where leaf colour is lightening one dilute feed will, in a few days, bring improvement and darkening of the green in the leaves and then we know we are on the right track and additional fertiliser can be given. A little and often is the golden rule, not occasional great injections of concentrated doses.

Plants which make excessive leaf growth at the expense of flower may be over fed. Such plants are certainly better given liquid feeds high in potash, for example liquid tomato fertiliser. Where the reverse is the case and leaf growth is hard and slow with the leaves comparatively small, the fertilisers high in nitrogen are needed. The proprietary house plant foods have ample nitrogen for the last mentioned condition.

Pruning

Many of the evergreen foliage plants used for indoor decoration can be regenerated and made more bushy by a little pruning. This is especially the case with the climbers. Taking the regeneration of old plants first, the opportunity here is to cut back quite hard where plants have lost their lower leaves and look more like palms in the desert than attractive house plants. Very often new growth will come from low down and a new specimen, furnished with leaves from the base, can be grown. If you have plants which are no longer attractive it is well worth the risk of cutting hard back and spring is invariably the best time to do this.

Less aggressive pruning is needed on young plants where the plan is to remove just the growing tip to encourage a number of branches to sprout from the base of the plant. This is important with climbing and trailing plants, where a mass of attractive growth is the aim rather than one very long, straggling shoot.

Where bulbs are grown in containers without drainage the special 'bulb fibre' should be selected for the growing compost. Bulb fibre is

Growing Bulbs in Pots and Bowls

1

2

3

4

1. Hyacinth bulbs being 'screwed' into a bowl filled with well moistened bulb fibre. Screwing in helps reduce the tendency for bulbs to lift as the new roots push downwards.

2. Fill the bowl with bulbs, making sure the bulbs do not touch.

3. To avoid placing decorative bowls outside, use peat pots to grow to the bringing indoors stage.

4. 5. Plant and roots grow through the peat pot and can subsequently be bowled up with a little extra compost.

5

6

7

8

6. 7. 8. The first layer of Narcissus in two layer planting to get more flowers from a given pot size. The 15 cm (6 in) pot planted with two layers.

predominantly peat but has both charcoal and oyster-shell added to keep the peat sweet, that is, not acrid from excessive water and lack of air caused by growing in a container which is not free draining. Any of the potting composts can be used in all containers from peat pots to the ordinary flower pot which allow excessive water to drain out of the base.

When planting in bulb fibre first ensure the peat is moist. Warm water can be introduced to dry compost more easily than cold. The correct moisture level can be checked by squeezing a handful, if the fibre is damp enough moisture will just ooze from the fingers. Once this is done all you need to do is loosely fill the bowl and give it a tap to settle, then screw the bulbs into the compost by giving a one-half circular turn. As the bulbs are pushed in sufficient firming is provided.

Once bowled and potted most bulbs need a period of cool, dark conditions to produce roots and shoots before bringing indoors, when leaves and flowers develop and mature. This is especially important for the majority of spring flowering bulbs potted in the autumn. Placing the filled containers outside and covering with several inches of peat is the best way of giving this cool, root forming period.

Plant crocus bowls with corm and shoot poking out from the sides.

Cleaning plants

Dust and dirt falls on the leaves of indoor plants as it does on everything else and for the plants' well being as well as its appearance, the occasional wash and brush up is advisable. Plants with a smooth and shiny surface to the leaves are easy, here it is just a matter of occasionally wiping the leaves over with a damp cloth or sponge. If you like a real lustre to the leaves then once every few months, after washing, apply a thin film of proprietary leaf shine material. Make sure the plants are well watered and the compost nicely damp before applying leaf shine. Don't over do the leaf shine, the occasional application is all you need. Some people use a mixture of half milk and half water for leaf shine, but I have found the specially formulated leaf shine materials a better bet.

Plants with smaller leaves and especially the larger specimens may take too long to wipe by hand and here one simple way is to lie the plant on its side in the bath and give the foliage a good shower. Taking such specimens outside and syringing well with water is another easy method.

Plants with furry and fluffy foliage are best brushed over with a soft paint brush and once this is done, a fine syringing with water will not come amiss as long as they are in an atmosphere where the leaves are dry again within 24 hours.

Sponging the leaves with a damp cloth cleans away dust and increases humidity around the plant.

Pests and Diseases

The control of pest and disease for any one plant is covered in the specific plant description, but there are one or two general pieces of advice worth remembering. Plants growing strongly in the right compost, moisture levels and situation are seldom troubled by pest and disease.

Where a build-up of the ever present greenfly (aphis) occurs we can either water the compost with a systemic pest killer — that is a chemical taken up by the roots and transmitted throughout the plant — which will give control for quite a period, or spray the foliage. Where sprays are used I believe the easiest system is to take the plant outside and place in a large polythene bag, spray the plant and then close up the bag for a short time. In the case of aerosols it is just a matter of giving a short squirt into the bag and sealing up.

Hot, dry atmospheres encourage the build up of red spider. This tiny insect can just about be seen on the underside of the leaves and when present in large numbers produces thin webbing. Leaves invariably take on a paler colour and have a bronzed appearance. Regular syringing to increase humidity deters this pest and the best in home spray control is Derris.

A number of the more woody perennial plants, especially the evergreens, are attacked by scale and mealy bug insects. The scale insect is identified by the presence of small orangey-brown waxy scales about 0.5 cm (¼ in) across on the underside of leaves. The mealy bug is of similar size and has fluffy white covering. A quick cure for these is to wrap some cottonwool around the end of a match, dip this in methylated spirit and wipe the pests off with this.

There are two common diseases of house plants, the grey mould and soft, wet, brown rots of botrytis, best controlled by avoiding excessive moisture on susceptible leaves and stems in cool conditions, and the white, powdery growth on leaves caused by mildew. Both diseases are controlled by the chemicals based on Benomyl.

Naming

This is how the correct Latin names are built up:-

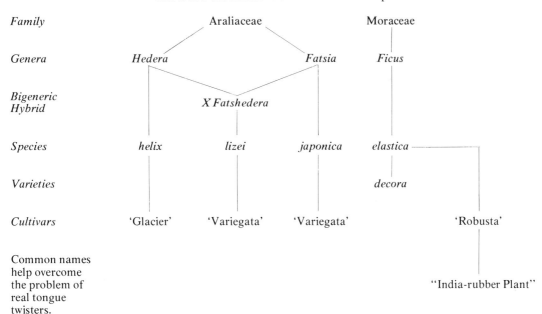

Family	Araliaceae		Moraceae
Genera	Hedera	Fatsia	Ficus
Bigeneric Hybrid	X Fatshedera		
Species	helix	lizei	japonica	elastica
Varieties				decora
Cultivars	'Glacier'	'Variegata'	'Variegata'	'Robusta'

Common names help overcome the problem of real tongue twisters.

"India-rubber Plant"

The difference between varieties and cultivars is simply the occurrence of varieties in the wild and cultivars under cultivation.

There is a wide choice of pot plant holders, with different kinds for various styles of furniture.

Plant display

The pots for plants are perfectly practical but in many cases hardly decorative. We have today a very wide range of pot plant holders and pot plant covers which can add considerably to the attractiveness of plants. One need not restrict use to the purpose made containers when many household objects are even more decorative. Deep bronze foliage and scarlet flowers are attractive in antique copper containers, the early spring flowering primroses have a pleasant natural appearance in rustic containers covered by bark. A glass goldfish bowl is a good resting place for a *Saintpaulia* and the trailing plants are attractive in the woven split cane baskets. There is no limit to the possibilities, given a little thought and imagination.

There are many plants which require either support for their climbing and trailing stems or containers constructed to allow the growth to trail from above. Where climbers are grown to form free-standing specimens some central means of support is needed. The most simple and least obvious is a piece of green split cane with the stems held in position by wire or plastic plant rings. One can also buy plastic and cane ladders, just push the base into the compost and the plant clambers over and through the ladder support.

A plastic ladder support (left) and single green split cane (right) used to support ivy.

Generally we are looking for a support system which will be completely hidden by the growing plant. Both the semi rigid plastic netting and plastic coated wire netting are suitable for this. Where the plant produces aerial roots, especially the larger specimens, the two kinds of net can be rolled to form a cylinder and filled with either sphagnum moss or peat. The roll of netting must be introduced at the time of potting on so that the bottom of the roll can be buried in the compost and gain strength to remain upright.

Some retailers offer specially made green plastic hoops which are ideal for supporting the climbing and twining species. Once the plant is well established the support is hidden under the foliage.

Ornamental wall brackets are available to display trailing plants and it is advisable to select the kinds with a built in saucer if water marks on walls are to be avoided.

The green plastic hoop supporting the trailing Asparagus stems is hidden from view (left) and plastic wire netting has been introduced to support the ivy (right).

Brackets with saucers to prevent water drips are advisable.

There is a wide range of wall brackets available, including a number made of cane.

The bracket is virtually hidden as the trailing plant develops.

One very attractive way to use house plants is to arrange a group which have complimentary colour and form in either a dish or bowl. Select an attractive container of your own, alternatively buy one, take it to your local house plant centre and arrange a collection of plants of your choice in it. If you wish, the plants can be left in their individual pots surrounded by damp peat. It is more common practice to take plants from the pot and actually plant in the bowl, allowing the four or five specimens to grow together.

Arrange taller specimens to the back or centre of the bowl and trailing kinds round the edge. Where one flowering plant is featured in the front of such an arrangement, it is as well to make provision to remove the plant once flowering is over and replace it with another flowering specimen. The foliage plants usually outlive the flower life of any one flowering plant.

It can be seen from these illustrations how quickly and easily a mixed bowl arrangement can be selected and made up. The plants illustrated gave months of pleasure with the planted bowl standing on a low table close to a north facing window. *(See picture on page 127.)*

Plants of different height, form, leaf colour and habit are selected and arranged in the bowl.

Some compost is placed in the bowl and planting commences with the tallest specimen.

Fit each plant into its respective position and fill in with compost.

Invert the plant and knock the base of the pot with the palm of the hand to remove.

When complete water and place in light position.

left: Hypocyrta glabra
back: Philodendron scandens
centre: Hedera 'Goldchild'
right: Peperomia magnifoliaefolia 'Variegata'